UNIX Fundamentals: UNIX for DOS and Windows Users

■ ■ ■

by Kevin Reichard

A Subsidiary of
Henry Holt and Co., Inc.

First Edition—1994

Printed in the United States of America.

Library of Congress Cataloging-in-Publication Data

Reichard, Kevin.
    UNIX fundamentals. UNIX for DOS and windows users/Kevin Reichard.
       p.   cm.
    Includes index.
    ISBN 1-55828-361-7
    1. UNIX (Computer file) 2. Operating systems (Computers)
I. Title.
QA76.76.063R444   1994
005.4'3--dc20   94-37373
                                              CIP

10 9 8 7 6 5 4 3 2 1

MIS:Press books are available at special discounts for bulk purchases for sales promotions, premiums, fund-raising, or educational use. Special editions or book excerpts can also be created to specification.

For details contact: Special Sales Director
                       MIS:Press
                       a subsidiary of Henry Holt and Company, Inc.
                       115 West 18th Street
                       New York, New York 10011

Publisher: Brenda McLaughlin   Associate Production Editor: Erika Putre
Development Editor: Laura Lewin   Technical Editor: Eric Johnson
Production Editor: Patricia Wallenburg   Copy Editor: Suzanne Ingrao

▪ **DEDICATION** ▪

As always—for Penny, Sean, and Geisha

▪ TABLE OF CONTENTS ▪

▼

▼

▪ INTRODUCTION ▪

Welcome to *UNIX For DOS/Windows Users!* As a DOS and/or *Windows* user, you're in for an interesting transition. But an operating system is an operating system, right? Wrong—especially when it comes to DOS and UNIX.

While the two may share some superficial similarities, the two differ when it comes to their basic computing orientation. DOS was written for a single-user personal computer, while UNIX was written for a multiuser minicomputer. These roots show through to the present user base: The majority of DOS users work on standalone PCs (indeed, DOS runs on *nothing* but a personal computer), while UNIX users are all over the map. Virtually any type of computer—ranging from personal computers like IBM PS/2s, Apple Macintoshes, and Compaq Presarios to Sun Microsystems workstations to DEC minicomputers to Cray Research supercomputers—runs the UNIX operating system. As such, it's one of the most popular operating systems on the face of the earth, as some market-research firms estimate that there are over 80 million UNIX users.

▼

Who Should Read This Book?

Obviously, this book was intended for the DOS/*Windows* user who wants to learn about the UNIX operating system. This still covers a lot of ground, and so this book is geared toward those who have:

▲ Worked extensively with DOS and/or *Windows* and are moving up to UNIX as the result of changes in the workplace

▲ Supported DOS and *Windows* in a corporate or educational atmosphere but now must also supports UNIX

▲ Some previous limited experience with DOS and are learning more about UNIX for various reasons

▲ Purchased PCs running DOS and *Windows* but are now looking at UNIX as an alternative

▲ Made a commitment to computing and are trying to decide between DOS and UNIX

With this kind of audience in mind, this book was written taking nothing for granted in terms of experience and expertise. Beginning UNIX concepts—even those with direct counterparts in the DOS world—are explained on a very basic level. The very nature of UNIX and what makes it so unique (like security, networking, multiuser, and multitasking features) is told through these basic concepts.

Command Comparisons

When a new UNIX command is introduced, you'll also find a Command Reference within the same section. These references exist for two reasons: They summarize the main points from the text, and they also are designed to stand out when you inevitably return to the text to review information about a command or procedure. The Command Reference will use the same layout throughout the book:

▲ **Command syntax.** This details exactly how you use the command. The syntax of commands is explained in more detail in Chapter 1.

▲   **Purpose.** One or two sentences summarize what the command does.

▲   **Options.** Virtually every command features options, which change the way the command works. Again, commands and options are covered in detail in Chapter 1.

When direct comparisons are made between DOS and UNIX commands, there will be a table listing both commands, their purpose, and switches and options for each command. (See Chapter 2 for an explanation of switches and options as they relate to commands.)

Since some of the UNIX commands have rather lengthy lists of options—including many options that are rarely used—some discretion was used when compiling lists of commands and options. You shouldn't assume that the listings of options cover every possible option; otherwise, this book would have been even bigger than it is now. If you're interested in complete command references, check Appendix A for a listing of UNIX reference works.

Examples in This Book

There are many examples used within this book to illuminate concepts and practices. With every UNIX system being different, there's the real danger that the examples cannot be used by every UNIX end user. However, always remember that even if the specific example isn't applicable to your specific situation, the general concepts behind the example are applicable to the vast majority of UNIX systems. For instance, something as mundane as logging in a UNIX system varies from system to system. However, virtually every UNIX system requires a login procedure of one form or another. In this instance, what's important is not the actual set of keystrokes that logs you in a system, but the procedure of logging in a system and the concepts behind the need for logins.

Reality Checks

Throughout this book, UNIX usage will be treated in two ways: The ways things should work in theory, and the way things sometimes work in the real world—or not work, as the case may be. For instance, the opening chapter of this book deals with the nasty fact that things can go wrong with something as mundane as logging on a system, and what you should do if something goes wrong. The way things usually work is detailed in special sections entitled "Reality Checks," which will detail how you should deal with the times when UNIX doesn't quite work the way it should.

Icons

Important UNIX concepts and commands are highlighted with icons from the artist John Bush (who is also responsible for the illustrations at the beginning of each chapter). There are several different icons used:

Command, which points out where a UNIX command is introduced and explained

Note This, which highlights an important fact or concept

Take Your Time, which tells you not to worry about why things work—just that they should work

This is Technical, which explains a more technical issue

Conventions Used in This Book

Many of the things discussed in this book will be confusing to you, and sometimes the way books are laid out adds to the confusion. We've attempted to create a very user-friendly book to help you wade through the very confusing world of UNIX computing. Some of the things we've done include:

▲ Commands that are to be typed directly into the UNIX system are indicated by the `monospaced` font.

▲ Keystrokes—that is, keys you press as part of your UNIX system usage, such as the **Enter** key—are indicated by **bold** type.

▲ Filenames and directories are also in **bold** type.

▲ Machine names and electronic-mail addresses are marked by the *italic* type.

▲ New concepts are introduced and highlighted in *italic* type.

UNIX Fundamentals

This book is one in a series of books from MIS:Press, UNIX Fundamentals, dedicated toward UNIX end users. This series is an ambitious attempt to explain the UNIX operating system in terms the average end user can handle. This is more of a project than you might think—the vast majority of offerings in the UNIX-book world center around advanced technical information for system administrators and UNIX gurus.

If you find yourself curious about UNIX after reading this book, you should check out some of the other titles in the series. The first title, *UNIX Basics*, covers the UNIX operating system from the ground up. Other titles in the series focus on electronic mail/networking/ Internet and UNIX freeware/shareware.

Acknowledgments

Many people were central in bringing this book to your hands:

- ▲ **Laura Lewin**, a very patient editor who is responsible for the look and feel of the entire series; she deserves far more credit for bringing this book (and, indeed, the UNIX Fundamentals series) to a successful publication than she'll ever receive.

- ▲ **Nelson King**, MIS:Press author and a frequent coffee companion who sagacious advice helped shape this work.

- ▲ The members of the CompuServe UNIX Forum (particularly George L. Smythe and Caroll Ford), who provide a very useful window in the world of UNIX users.

Feedback

I'd love to hear your comments about this book—good, bad, or ugly. If you're connected in some way to the Internet (don't worry if you have no idea about what this means—you'll cover the Internet and electronic mail in Chapter 7), you can send me electronic mail at *kreichard@mcimail.com*. If you have a CompuServe account, you can drop me a note there (my account number is 73670,3422). Or, if your UNIX system is not connected to the Internet, you can drop me a line in care of MIS:Press, 115 W. 18th St., New York City, NY 10011.

▪ CHAPTER ONE ▪
Introducing UNIX

The operating system controls all portions of the computer system. In this respect UNIX and DOS work the same: They take instructions from you and translate the commands into something the computer can understand. Past this, however, there are some key differences between DOS and UNIX, as you'll see through coverage of the following topics:

▲ An overview of UNIX

▲ The multiuser aspects of the UNIX operating system

▲ The multitasking aspects of the UNIX operating system

▲ UNIX development through the ages

▲ Various versions of UNIX from various vendors

▲ Terminals and how they are used by UNIX

▲ An overview of the X Window System

▲ Introducing OSF/Motif

▲ Window managers and the X Window System

▲ OSF/Motif compared directly to Microsoft *Windows*

▲ The Motif Window Manager

▲ Other window managers, such as the Open Look Window Manager and the Tab Window Manager

Moving Up to UNIX

An operating system is an operating system, right? Wrong—especially when it comes to a comparison of UNIX and DOS.

If you're an experienced DOS or *Windows* user, you'll find that a move up to UNIX isn't as complicated as you anticipated. Many of DOS's foundations—the file structure, the use of commands—are the same as UNIX's foundations. And there are many similarities between Microsoft *Windows* and the X Window System—at least as far as the user is concerned.

Indeed, DOS at one time was based on UNIX, at least in the way it was designed to interact with users. The original version of DOS, as developed by Seattle Computer (*not* Microsoft—Microsoft bought the rights to DOS from Seattle Computer) was built to look like UNIX in many ways, especially when it came to files, directories, and the command line. But from the beginning there were other more serious differences between DOS and UNIX, differences that persist to this day. These include:

▲ **Single-user versus multiuser.** DOS was designed to serve the needs of one user on a personal computer. UNIX was designed to work with multiple users all connected via terminals to a central computer.

When you're logged on a UNIX system via a terminal, you can approach the system as if you're the only user on the system. You don't need to acknowledge other users or worry about using the same files. The UNIX operating system does all the dirty work when it comes to managing multiple users.

However, the need to support multiple users does add a level of complexity to the UNIX operating system that is not found or not widely used in DOS or *Windows*. There are issues surrounding security and who exactly has access to what files, as well as safeguards used to prevent unauthorized usage of the UNIX system.

▲ **Single tasking versus multitasking.** DOS does one thing at a time. UNIX, on the other hand, is **multitasking** and therefore can run more than one program at a time. Users can launch multiple programs—or **processes**—and then switch between them, assigning priorities to the processes and suspending those that are not a high priority. This is such an integral part of the UNIX computing experience—and one with limited comparisons with the DOS/*Windows* world—that Chapter 5 is devoted to multitasking.

Windows, too, can also run more than one program at a time, although it doesn't handle them in the same manner as UNIX does. Instead, *Windows* switches between programs; only one program is actually running, while the rest are present in memory. Since newer microchips like the Intel 486 and Pentium are so powerful, the switching between programs is so fast that most users think that they are actually running simultaneously. But at the core, there's only one program actually running.

As this book was written, the next generation of Microsoft *Windows*—code-named *Chicago*—was not yet released. Therefore, the comments about *Windows* throughout this book will apply to version 3.1.

▲   **Complex versus simple.** UNIX developed haphazardly throughout the ages. When a new feature was desired, someone would merely hack out a new command and then add it to their own particular version of UNIX. Adding a new command here and there didn't really matter, as most UNIX implementations were running on larger minicomputers or mainframes. And since no central authority oversaw UNIX development for the benefit of the entire UNIX computing community, commands could be added willynilly. Such anarchical development has led to a woefully complex operating system, however—there are literally hundreds of UNIX commands, some arising in response to specific situations, and others that have been adapted and expanded for new uses. There are many, many UNIX commands that do the same thing—or nearly the same thing. And it's led to a situation where there—at least at one time—were hundreds of versions of the UNIX operating system floating around in the marketplace. (See "An Aside: UNIX Versions," for more information.)

By contrast, DOS development has always been overseen by Microsoft Corp., as has *Windows* development. Because changes to the operating system were always taken more seriously in the DOS/*Windows* world than they were in the UNIX world, new commands and tools were added only when they would benefit the majority of users, not merely a few. And since development took place under a centralized system, upgrades were serious matters, occurring less than once a year.

▲ **Support staff.** Since a UNIX installation tends to be a rather involved operation, many companies assign employees to oversee the network. These employees, called **system administrators**, are in charge of the entire system. They add users, delete accounts, monitor disk usage, and in general make sure the system runs smoothly and efficiently. Being a UNIX system administrator is a specialized task, and many corporations seek system administrators who have been accredited on some level.

On the other hand, you're in charge of your PC (generally speaking) running DOS. Sure, your company may have computer support staff, but this support staff isn't going to be devoted to your own personal computer. In these cases, you need to take a certain level of responsibility for what happens on your computer. You need to make sure your hard drive isn't crammed to the gills with unnecessary files. You need to make sure that sensitive data is hidden from unauthorized users. And you need to make sure that your software is working properly.

Today there's a higher level of interaction between DOS/*Windows* and UNIX than you might expect. Today's advanced networks make it easy to connect a network of DOS-based computers with a network of UNIX-based computers. Software like *DESQview/X* allows you to connect a DOS-based PC to a UNIX network and run DOS and *Windows* programs from the UNIX terminals. And most versions of UNIX for the PC allow you to run DOS and *Windows* sessions while running UNIX as the main operating system.

Why Learn About the Operating System?

These days the goal of many system administrators and other computer-support specialists is to remove the user from direct interaction with the operating system. In theory, the operating system exists only to run programs, and users should be using these programs, not the operating system directly. That's why we have things like *Windows* and the X Window System: These programs hide many operating-system procedures—and particularly, the command line—from the likes of you, the average user.

Still, there are many operations that are easier when done from the command line. Anything to do with files and directories, for instance, can be easier when done from the command line than from a file browser or file manager. Direct access to the command line is still an important fact in the UNIX world: The most popular X Window application is **xterm**, a terminal emulator that presents a UNIX prompt.

This chapter introduces the UNIX operating system, as well as the X Window System, a popular graphical interface.

What is UNIX?

Like DOS, UNIX is an operating system. It controls all aspects of the computer system, taking instructions from the user and translating the instructions into something the computer understands. When you print a file, you're telling the operating system to print the file. When you edit a file, you're first calling an application through the operating system, which then loads the file into memory.

As mentioned in the previous section, UNIX is a multiuser operating system. This is perhaps UNIX's greatest strength when it comes to corporate decisions to adopt UNIX. With UNIX, networking is built into the operating system, and the assumption is that UNIX will indeed be used within a network.

This network can be set up many different ways. One popular method is to attach a number of **terminals** to a UNIX **server**, hence allowing the server to distribute files and services, such as printing. This sort of setup is shown in Figure 1.1.

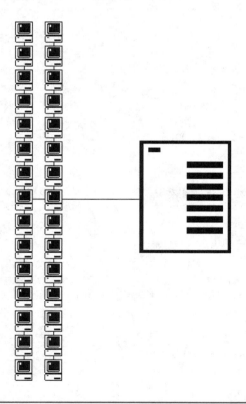

FIGURE 1.1 A typical **UNIX** network built around a server.

Another great strength of the UNIX operating system is that it is **modular** in nature. One UNIX network can be connected to another UNIX network. When all is said and done, the end user won't need to know that there are separate UNIX networks—it will appear to be one large **filesystem**, even when portions of the network are housed in different buildings or even different states. Companies can add separate networks to the larger network, all without requiring an overhaul of the entire network or the operating system. In fact, UNIX even allows non-UNIX operating systems to be tied into a UNIX network. The ease of this action depends on the non-UNIX operating system being added, of course; Novell, for instance, has taken great pains in order to maximize UNIX-*NetWare* interoperability. This type of networking scheme is illustrated by Figure 1.2, where two servers are connected.

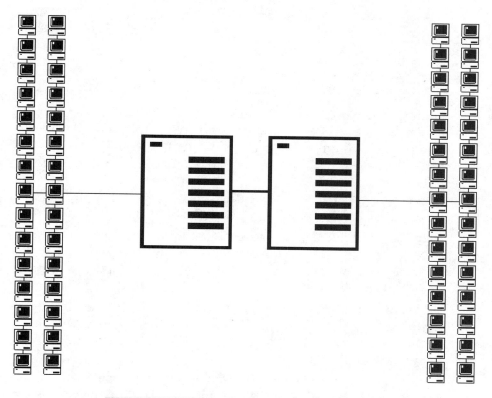

FIGURE 1.2 A UNIX network with connected servers.

Of course, UNIX doesn't need a server to allow communication between terminals. Many smaller UNIX implementations merely connect UNIX terminals. A department at a university or college, for instance, will typically just connect a series of workstations and share information between them, without the need for a dedicated server. A network of this sort is shown in Figure 1.3.

FIGURE 1.3 A small UNIX network.

UNIX Versions

Rumor—or urban folklore—has it that at one time there were over 200 implementation of UNIX on the market. While there's no way to confirm or disprove this number (indeed, why bother?), it does illustrate the wide range of UNIX implementations that have hit the market in recent history.

This is due mainly to UNIX's somewhat checkered past in the marketplace. UNIX was originally developed by Bell Labs. At that time, AT&T was prohibited by the government from offering computer software or services. Since AT&T could not legally sell UNIX, AT&T gave UNIX away. Since universities are always in the market for freebies, many universities started using UNIX and then made changes to it.

Eventually there was East Coast UNIX (with roots in the AT&T version of UNIX) and West Coast UNIX (reflecting enhancements made at the University of California at Berkeley). Some commands were found only in one flavor of UNIX.

However, the UNIX industry righted itself through UNIX System Laboratories—first owned by AT&T and then sold to Novell, the creators of the popular PC network operating system *NetWare*—and embarked on the Grand Unification of UNIX. Features from West Coast and East Coast UNIX were combined into the newest version of UNIX, System V Release 4.

This is technical

Still, there's not 100 percent uniformity in the UNIX world. Each vendor likes to differentiate its UNIX wares: IBM has AIX, Hewlett-Packard has HP-UX, Sun Microsystems has both SunOS and Solaris, DEC has both Ultrix and OSF/1, and so on. The rule of thumb is that vendors aren't forced to support every UNIX command or tool.

Though most of the major UNIX commands can be found in every mainstream UNIX implementation, there are many marginal tools and practices that are not universal. And file locations *definitely* vary from vendor to vendor.

As far as you are concerned, all of this is slightly interesting background on a popular operating system. The lesson to be learned has to do with one simple truth: Nothing is guaranteed on every UNIX system. The examples in this book should be applicable to most popular versions of UNIX, but don't be surprised if the commands work slightly different on your UNIX system, or that many files are stored in different file locations.

What is a Terminal?

In essence, a terminal is the computer hardware that you use to access the UNIX system. Some older UNIX texts refer to the terminal as the **console**. In many ways, the terminal—as viewed by the UNIX operating system—is an abstraction that represents many different hardware configurations. This is due to the very nature of the UNIX operating system as it's been implemented.

With DOS and *Windows*, there's actually a limited range of hardware configurations (relatively speaking) that run the DOS operating system: personal computers built around an Intel microprocessor (or clone). In some cases, Apple Macintoshes can be configured to run DOS, either through software emulation or through an Intel chip contained on a separate board. But these Macs are not prevalent in the marketplace and do not represent a sizable number of DOS and *Windows* users.

However, a much wider range of computers can run the UNIX operating system. In fact, virtually every type of computer—ranging from PCs, Apple Macintoshes, and Commodore Amigas on the low end to Cray Research supercomputers on the high end—can run the UNIX operating system. For instance, this book is being written on a PC running UnixWare, a version of UNIX for the PC from Novell. This version of UNIX features all of the major UNIX commands, as well as the X Window System and networking capabilities.

Because UNIX is not limited to a single hardware type, the generic reference to the hardware used by the user is the terminal. Depending on the type of computer running the UNIX operating system, the terminal can be many things. A terminal may be a **dumb terminal**, which has relatively limited computing power and draws most of its computing power from the UNIX server. A terminal may be a UNIX **workstation**, a relatively powerful (and relatively expensive) computer optimized to run UNIX. (SPARCstations from Sun and RS/6000s from IBM are all examples of workstations.) A terminal may be an **X terminal**, a computer optimized for running the X Window System; while there may be some computing power locally within the X terminal, most of the X terminal's computing power is drawn from the UNIX server. And, of course, a terminal can be a personal computer built around an Intel microprocessor, either running UNIX on its own, a terminal emulator (software that makes the PC look like a dumb terminal as far as the UNIX server is concerned), or an X server that (like an X terminal) draws most of its power from the server.

As you can see, that's a wide range of hardware. Because of this, there are generic references to a terminal. Generally speaking, a terminal consists of a monitor, a keyboard, and (if the UNIX system is running the X Window System) a mouse. A typical terminal setup is shown in Figure 1.4.

Of course, chances are that your terminal will look different than what is shown in Figure 1.4. That's the point—every terminal will look different, but at its core the UNIX system will assume that you have a keyboard for inputting commands and a monitor for reading the commands and the results of the commands. This book assumes that your own terminal features a monitor, a keyboard, and a mouse.

FIGURE 1.4 A UNIX terminal (as far as the system is concerned).

The X Window System

An important tool for many UNIX users these days is the **X Window System**, a **graphical interface** first developed at the Massachusetts Institute of Technology and now under the guidance of the not-for-profit X Consortium, Inc.

A graphical interface, in essence, puts a friendlier face on UNIX. Instead of leaving you at the mercies of the command line, a graphical interface uses windows, icons, and the mouse to present computing choices. For instance: Instead of typing **vi** at a command line to launch the popular **vi** text editor, a UNIX system running the X Window System would have an icon representing a text editor (probably **xedit**), which you would click on with your mouse to launch.

If you've used *Windows*, you know what the X Window System is all about. Both have the same goals in mind: They provide an easier-to-use environment to an operating system that can be difficult to use. Instead of interacting directly with the operating system (see Chapter 2 for more on this interaction), *Windows* and the X Window System hides the messy details. Their roles in the computing experience are illustrated in Figure 1.5.

However, the X Window System and *Windows* differ on some key points. *Windows* is a total environment, complete with applications like a word processor (*Write*), a telecommunications package (*Terminal*), and a graphics editor (*Paintbrush*). On the other hand, at its core the X Window System is really a set of building blocks for more fully fleshed-out graphical environments. When X Window was first developed, its creators stressed *mechanism*, not *policy*. This distinction, as translated into something meaningful for end users, means that most users won't actually use the X Window System directly, but one of many implementations built on top of the X Window System.

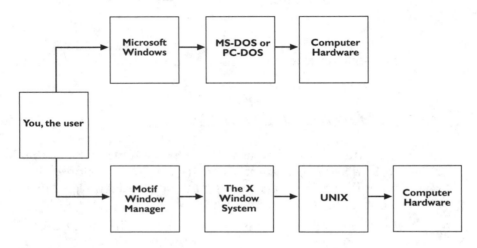

FIGURE 1.5 The computing process.

One of the most popular flavors, and the flavor that will become the de facto style in the UNIX world, is called OSF/Motif. Developed by the Open Software Foundation (OSF), OSF/Motif encompasses many things. However, as far as you are concerned, OSF/Motif manifests itself through the Motif Window Manager, or **mwm**, which is shown in Figure 1.6.

A **window manager** controls the look-and-feel of the elements on the screen. (You never actually interact with the X Window System or OSF/Motif; you interact with the window manager.) The window manager determines the size of windows and the decorations surrounding the windows (such as the buttons on the top-left and top-right of the window). A window manager is just like any other UNIX program, however, subject to the same rules that every program must acknowledge.

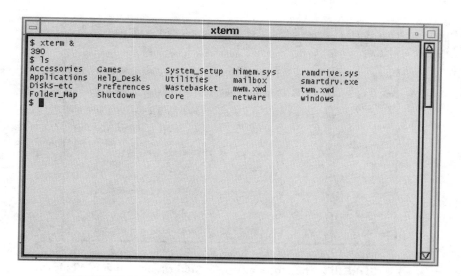

```
$ xterm &
390
$ ls
Accessories   Games         System_Setup    himem.sys      ramdrive.sys
Applications  Help_Desk     Utilities       mailbox        smartdrv.exe
Disks-etc     Preferences   Wastebasket     mwm.xwd        twm.xwd
Folder_Map    Shutdown      core            netware        windows
$ ▌
```

FIGURE 1.6 A window running under the Motif Window Manager.

Additions to Windows

This is technical

There are analogies to the window manager in the *Windows* world. Though Microsoft designed *Windows* to be the main source of interaction between the user and the computer system, other vendors have come out with the software that is used in conjunction with *Windows*, yet they present a different look and feel to users. Hewlett-Packard has developed *New Wave*, software that allows icons to be dragged and dropped to facilitate actions like printing and file management. Xerox's *Rooms*, Central Point Software's *PC Tools*, and Symantec's *Norton Desktop* each presents a different look and feel in the *Windows* environment, managing multiple applications and keeping track of several projects at once. All of these radically change the way you interact with *Windows*.

Compare Figure 1.6 to Figure 1.7, which shows the *Notepad* application running in *Windows*.

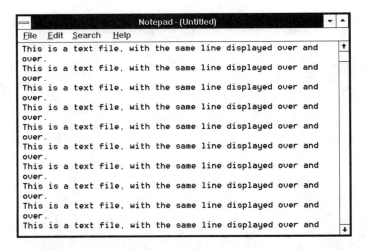

FIGURE 1.7 The Notepad application running under Windows.

While at first glance the two windows would appear to be quite different, there are many similarities between the two. Both contain a hidden Window Menu at the top-left corner; if you place your cursor over the area and press your left mouse button, a window will appear. Both contain a **titlebar** stretching across the top of the window; if you place your cursor over the titlebar and press on your left mouse button, you can then drag the window to a new location on the screen. Both contain Minimize and Maximize buttons on the top-right corner: The Minimize button replaces the window with a icon on the bottom of the screen when pressed, and the Maximize button will resize the window to its maximum size when pressed. And both feature **scrollbars** on the right side of the screen, used to move the document up and down.

There's one big difference between Figure 1.6 and Figure 1.7: The *Windows* window features a menubar beneath the titlebar (**File**, **Edit**, **Search**, and **Help**). The **xterm** window does not. This is due to an inconsistency within the **xterm** application, not due to any style considerations with OSF/Motif or the X Window System. Almost all OSF/Motif applications feature a menubar—at least the OSF/Motif applications that follow the style guide.

These similarities are no accident. Both *Windows* and the Motif Window Manager generally conform to what are called the Common User Access (CUA) guidelines from IBM. In addition to the Motif Window Manager and *Windows*, IBM's own OS/2 also conforms to CUA guidelines.

The decorations for the **xterm** window, which was first shown in Figure 1.6, are illustrated in Figure 1.8.

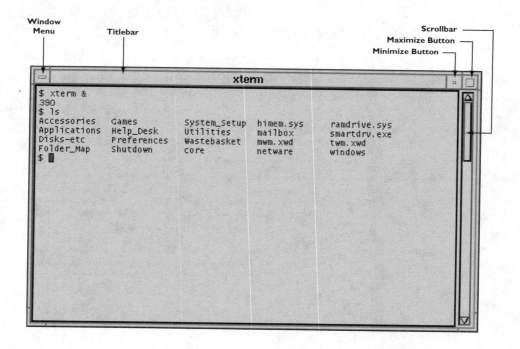

FIGURE 1.8 A mwm window illustrated.

Different vendors made subtle changes to the Motif Window Manager and then included the resulting window manager under a different name. However, at their core, these variants are running the Motif Window Manager. Some of the common variants are listed in Table 1.1.

TABLE 1.1 MOTIF WINDOW MANAGER VARIANTS.

Program	Vendor
dxwm	Digital Equipment Corp., used with DECwindows
4Dwm	Silicon Graphics Inc.
NCDwm	NCD
dtwm	COSE
vuewm	Hewlett-Packard

Of course, OSF/Motif is not the only implementation of the X Window System on the market, of course. For many years, there was a pitched battle between OSF/Motif (as implemented and pushed by Hewlett-Packard, IBM, and Digital Equipment Corp.) and OpenWindows (pushed by Sun Microsystems and AT&T), manifested through the Open Look Window Manager (shown in Figure 1.9).

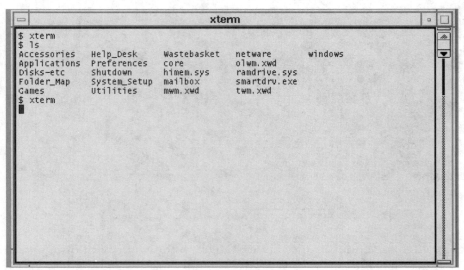

FIGURE 1.9 The Open Look Window Manager in action.

There are still many Open Look Window Manager (or **olwm**) users in the UNIX world, and you may indeed be one of them. However, Sun has announced that OSF/Motif will be the preferred interface of choice as part of the larger Common Open Software Environment offerings, which promises to make different versions of UNIX work more alike.

There's also the chance that you could be using the Tab Window Manager (**twm**), which ships with every implementation of the X Window System. As you can see from Figure 1.10, **twm** has a distinctive look.

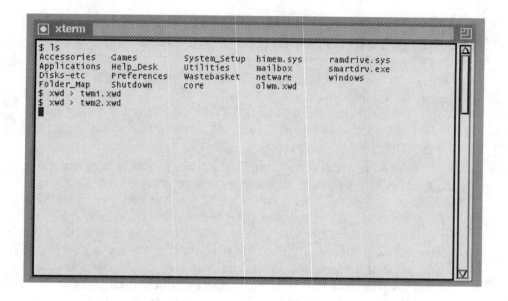

FIGURE 1.10 The Tab window manager.

From Figures 1.6, 1.9, and 1.10, you can see that that are many similarities between the three window managers. In theory, it is possible to move between them once you've mastered one. In reality, however, it's a little more difficult, as each window manager works a little differently, especially when it comes to the mouse and what the different mouse buttons do. (If you're used to using the Motif Window Manager, you'll be crossed up repeatedly if you switch to the Tab Window Manager, since the mouse-button actions are totally different between the two window managers.)

For the purposes of this book, it will be assumed that you're using the Motif Window Manager, since it is the most popular window manager on the market. Generally speaking, Window-Manager usage is determined for the entire system by the system administrator. However, there won't be a lot of discussion of specific **mwm** keystrokes or procedures, so much of the general discussion regarding **mwm** can be applied to any other window manager.

Matching Your System to Software

Like Windows and DOS, the combination of UNIX and the X Window System adds new requirements to software. Just as *Windows* software won't run on a PC containing DOS and not *Windows*, X Window System software won't run on a UNIX system that lacks a running copy of the X Window System.

However, generally speaking, in the UNIX world, you're not going to pick out your own personal software as you would in the DOS/*Windows* world, unless you're using UNIX on a standalone PC or workstation. UNIX software is generally more expensive than DOS/*Windows* software and usually must be implemented on a systemwide basis. It's usually not cost-effective to give one user one particular type of database-management software (like *Progress*) and then give other users another type of database-management software (like *Oracle*). In the UNIX world, you must make do with the software provided by the system administrator. And while most system administrators can be bribed with M&Ms for small favors (such as adding a freeware text editor like **emacs**), larger system decisions typically are not dictated by the needs of a single user.

This Chapter in Review

▲ The operating system controls the computer system and also translates your instructions into terms the computer system can understand.

▲   UNIX is an operating system, as is DOS from Microsoft. Some of the features of DOS, such as the file structure and the command line, are based on UNIX.

▲   However, there are other crucial differences between DOS and UNIX.

▲   UNIX is a multiuser system, which means that more than one user can be using the UNIX system at one time. DOS is a single-user operating system, which means only one user can be using DOS at a time.

▲   UNIX is a multitasking system, which means that multiple programs can be running simultaneously. DOS can only run one program at a time. *Windows* can manage multiple programs, although only one is running at a given time.

▲   The most popular graphical interface in the UNIX world is the X Window System, as well as a popular commercial product based on it: OSF/Motif.

▲   Most X Window System users will be using the Motif Window Manager (**mwm**). A window manager is a program that defines the look and feel of the windows on the screen, as well as overseeing interaction between the user and the operating system.

▲   In this sense, Microsoft *Windows* and the Motif Window Manager perform the same role (as far as users are concerned).

▲   Other popular window managers include the Open Look Window Manager (**olwm**) and the Tab Window Manager (**twm**).

▪ CHAPTER TWO ▪
Overview:
DOS/*Windows* versus UNIX/X

A s you delve into your UNIX and X Window System usage, you'll come to quickly realize that there are many similarities between them and DOS/*Windows*. Indeed, on the surface, the similarities are quite striking, and you'll probably be amazed at how quickly you can switch from DOS to UNIX. Some of the similarities, as covered in this chapter, include:

▲ The use of commands to directly address the system

▲ The use of command prompts by the system to tell you it's awaiting input

▲ The ability to change the characters used by the prompt

▲ The information returned by the DOS **DIR** and UNIX **ls** commands

▲ Using windows to get a direct access to a command prompt

▲ Using switches and options to modify a command

▲ Using command, switches, and options together to form a command line

▲ Using windows and icons with both *Windows* and the X Window System

▲ Using a titlebar and decorations to perform actions with windows

▲ Using the mouse cursor to make your way around the screen

▲ Using the mouse to select items on the screen

▲ Specific mouse actions that are used to perform tasks like moving and resizing windows

The More Things Change, The More They Stay the Same

As far as your personal interaction with UNIX goes, you're going to find that—procedurally, anyway—there's not as much difference between DOS and UNIX (or *Windows* and the X Window System, for that matter) as you might think. Both DOS and UNIX use **commands** to tell the computer systems exactly what to do. Both DOS and UNIX use a combination of commands and options to create a command line (which you'll learn about later in this chapter). And both DOS and UNIX vary in the methods they use when inputting these commands.

What is a command? In both DOS and UNIX, a command is a direct instruction to the computer system. You can't do a whole lot in either operating system if you don't know what a command is and how to use it.

The best way to explain commands is to use them in each operating system. There are some DOS commands that have direct counterparts in UNIX. (Appendix B lists the DOS command set—current as of MS-DOS 6.2—as well as the UNIX counterparts.)

One of the most commonly used commands in both DOS and UNIX involves listing the contents of a current directory.

In DOS, this command is called **DIR**. In UNIX, this command is called **ls**.

You've just collided with one major difference between DOS and UNIX. When you enter a command under DOS, the case of the specific letters doesn't matter. The DOS system treats **DIR**, **dir**, **Dir**, and **diR** the same: As a request to list the contents of the current directory. By contrast, UNIX *does* take the letter case seriously. A UNIX system would treat **ls**, **LS**, **Ls**, and **lS** as four separate commands.

Generally speaking, UNIX commands are lowercase, while the case of DOS commands doesn't matter. To distinguish between the two, UNIX commands will be lowercase—in the exact manner you should adopt when entering them in the system—and DOS commands will be listed in all uppercase.

Both DOS and UNIX support the use of **prompts** that tell you when the system is ready and waiting for a command, such as the aforementioned **DIR** and **ls**. With DOS, the standard prompt is:

>

as shown in a typical screen in Figure 2.1.

FIGURE 2.1 A typical DOS screen.

The prompt on a UNIX system works similarly. The exact symbol, however, depends on the **shell** currently in use. The two most common UNIX shells, the Bourne shell and the C shell, feature their own prompt symbols. In the case of the Bourne shell, the prompt is:

$

This is the same prompt used by the Korn shell, another popular UNIX prompt.

Don't worry about your current shell at the moment.

▲ L E A R N   M O R E   A B O U T ▲

You'll learn about shells in Chapter 5.

The C shell uses the following prompt:

`%`

or

`spike%`

where *spike* is the name of the computer. (In UNIX, computer systems have names. The reasons why will become evident when you read Chapter 6.) If you're using the Windowing Korn shell, your prompt will look like this:

`[WKSH]`

A typical UNIX screen is shown in Figure 2.2.

You'll learn more about prompts later in this chapter; for now, all you need to know is that both operating systems use prompts as a meant to solicit input from you.

Now that you know that the prompt is used to enter commands, you can use that knowledge and see how a command works.

FIGURE 2.2 A typical UNIX screen.

With DOS, you enter the command directly after the prompt. In this book, this action will be shown in the following manner:

`D:\> DIR`

This command yields output like the screen shot shown in Figure 2.3.

```
                            MS-DOS Prompt                    ▼ ▲
Microsoft<R> MS-DOS<R> Version 5.00
              (C)Copyright Microsoft Corp 1981-1991.

D:\WINDOWS>cd\kevin\books

D:\KEVIN\BOOKS>dir

 Volume in drive D has no label
 Volume Serial Number is 3479-11F2
 Directory of D:\KEVIN\BOOKS

.            <DIR>       04-29-94    6:06p
..           <DIR>       04-29-94    6:06p
ADVANCED     <DIR>       04-29-94    6:06p
UNIXDOS      <DIR>       05-01-94    9:07p
SHARE    DOC     10240   05-23-94    3:48p
PASICS           93283   05-24-94    9:00p
UNIXDOS  DOC      3897   05-30-94    2:24p
LAURA    DOC     12800   06-06-94    2:10p
UNIXCOMM     <DIR>       05-01-94    9:05p
BASICS       <DIR>       05-01-94    9:05p
        10 file<s>       120220 bytes
                      242581504 bytes free

D:\KEVIN\BOOKS>
```

FIGURE 2.3 The DIR command in action.

In this case, there were a few things done before the **DIR** command was run. But you get the general idea: The **DIR** command in DOS lists the contents of the current directory—both files and directories.

In UNIX, the **ls** command does the same thing, as you can see in Figure 2.4.

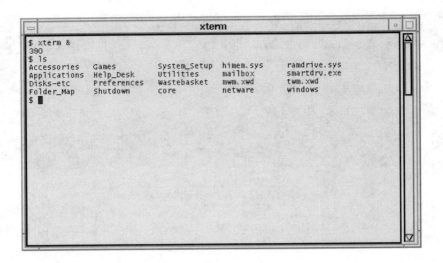

FIGURE 2.4 The ls command in action.

DIR and **ls** also share one more similarity: Their usage can be modified by the use of **options**, **command-line parameters**, **arguments**, and/or **switches**. Though there's different terminology in DOS and UNIX (DOS users will refer to command-line parameters and switches, while UNIX users will refer to options and arguments), the theory and usage is consistent in both operating systems: A command can be altered by the use of additional elements. The combination of the command and the elements becomes the **command line**.

Again, the best way to illustrate this is through the use of an example (or two or three), starting with the DOS **DIR** command. Though you probably haven't used these command-line parameters often in your DOS usage, they do exist.

```
D:\KEVIN\BOOKS> DIR /B

  Volume in drive D has no label
  Volume Serial Number is 3479-11F2
  Directory of D:\KEVIN\BOOKS


  [.]      [..]       [ADVANCED]   [UNIXDOS]   SHARE.DOC
  PASICS   UNIXDOS.DOC  LAURA.DOC   [UNIXCOMM]   [BASICS]
```

```
     10 file(s)      120220 bytes
                   242286592 bytes free
```

In this situation, the /*w* switch alters the **DIR** command, causing the output to be displayed in wide format (hence the *w*), and with only the filenames and directory names listed.

For the purposes of this discussion, you don't need to know anything about files and directories, past their existence.

▲ L E A R N   M O R E   A B O U T ▲

Chapter 3 will cover files and directories in both DOS and UNIX.

Going to the other extreme is the /*b* switch, which lists only the file and directory names:

```
D:\KEVIN\BOOKS> DIR /W
ADVANCED
UNIXDOS
SHARE.DOC
PASICS
UNIXDOS.DOC
LAURA.DOC
UNIXCOMM
BASICS
```

There are a number of switches available with the **DIR** command, as you can see in Table 2.1.

Still, generally speaking, most users don't use any switches with the **DIR** command, much less any DOS command. However, the use of options and arguments is integral to successful use of most UNIX commands. You'll see this with a quick review of the popular options to the **ls** command.

A plain vanilla use of the **ls** command will yield the barest amount of information possible:

```
$ ls
Accessories    Folder_Map    Preferences    Utilities     data
Applications   Games         Shutdown       Wastebasket   mailbox
Disks-etc      Help_Desk     System_Setup   core          netware
```

The columns are listed in alphabetical order (with capital letters listed before lowercase letters), in columnar form. On most UNIX systems, this will be the default. (If this is not the default on your system and you want to generate listings in this fashion, use the *-C* option.)

As you might be able to tell, this is the barest possible amount of information. Unlike the useful DOS **DIR** command—which delineates both files and directories as well as file sizes and times of creation—the UNIX **ls** command gives you the contents of the current directory with no additional information. You don't know what is a directory or what is a file. And, although you don't know it yet, you don't even have the full listings of the contents of the directory.

The generic **ls** command fails to list any **hidden** files. How do you hide a file? Simple—just give it a name beginning with a period (.), and the system will assume that the file is hidden; that is, not listing it during routine usage of the **ls** command. UNIX allows the creation of hidden files, which are used most often for standard housekeeping tasks by the system and applications. While DOS does feature hidden system files, they aren't as extensively used in DOS as they are in UNIX, and so their presence isn't as big a factor. But in UNIX, many applications, as well as the operating system, rely heavily on hidden files. Because there are times when you'll need to know about the existence of such hidden files (not to get ahead of ourselves here, but several commands in Chapter 3 will relate to the issue of hidden files), it's good to know how to generate a listing of *all* files. See the difference between the results of the generic **ls** command and the following:

```
$ ls -a
.               .lastsession  .profile      Games         Wastebasket
..              .login        .wastebasket  Help_Desk     core
.Xdefaults      .oliniterr    Accessories   Preferences   data
.dtfclass       .olinitout    Applications  Shutdown      mailbox
.dtinfo         .olinitrc     Disks-etc     System_Setup  netware
.dtprops        .olsetup      Folder_Map    Utilities
```

In this case, the *–a* option was used in conjunction with the **ls** command. The combination of **ls** and *–a* makes up a command line in the UNIX world.

You'll notice a fair amount of new files generated using the *–a* option. You'll also notice that the listing leads with . and ... These symbols are used to denote the current (.) directory and the parent (..) directory. Again, you'll learn more about this in the next chapter; the point here is to illustrate the usage of a command line, not to delve deeply into files and directories.

Both the DOS **DIR** and UNIX **ls** commands are explained further in Table 2.1. While the number of options associated with the **ls** command may be a little overwhelming, it's not atypical of the UNIX world. Indeed, it's a rare UNIX command that doesn't have any options; the more popular and useful the UNIX command is, generally speaking, the more available options it will have.

TABLE 2.1 COMPARISON OF THE DIR AND LS COMMANDS.

DIR	**ls**
Purpose	
List the files and directories in the current directory.	
Usage	
dir *path switches*	**ls** *options names*
Switches	**Options**
/B Displays only the file and directory names.	**–1** Lists one item per line.
/L Displays filenames in lowercase.	**–a** Lists all contents including hidden files.
/O:*o* Lists files in a specific order, as specified by *o* in one of the following options: **D** (chronological order), **E** (file extension, then name), **G** (by	**–c** Lists by creation/ modification time.
	–C Lists in columns (the default on the majority of UNIX systems).
	–d Lists only the name of

continued

Switches

subdirectory), **N** (filename), **S** (size).

/P Pause the scrolling display of names once the screen is filled.

/S Displays the files within the subdirectories.

/W Display the contents in wide format.

Options

the directory, not the contents.

–f Assume that *names* are directories, not files.

–F Flag executable filenames with an asterisk (*), directories with a slash (/), and symbolic links with @.

–g Lists in long form (see **–l**), omitting the owner of the file.

–l Lists the contents of a directory in long form.

–m Lists the contents across the screen, separated by commas.

–n Same as **-l**, except using numbers instead of names.

–o Same as **-l**, except the group name is omitted.

–p Displays a slash (/) at the end of every directory name.

–q Lists contents with non-printing characters represented by a question mark (?).

–r Lists the contents in reverse order.

continued

Switches	Options	
	–R	Recursively lists the contents of directories.
	–s	Lists file sizes in blocks, instead of the default bytes.
	–t	Lists the contents in order of time saved, beginning with the most recent.
	–x	Lists files in multi-column format.

More on the Prompt

As you learned earlier in this chapter, the prompt is the means by which both UNIX and DOS tell you that the system is ready and waiting for input. Quite often the prompt is changed by DOS users to provide a little more information. One of the commonest adaptations involves the following line placed in the **AUTOEXEC.BAT** file, which loads when the DOS system is booted and defines a number of procedures used by a PC:

```
PROMPT $p$g
```

The result of this line will yield the following prompt:

```
C:\DOS>
```

where *DOS* is the name of the current directory. When you change the current directory, you'll also change the information displayed on the prompt.

Don't worry about your current directory at the moment.

Take Your time

▲ L E A R N   M O R E   A B O U T ▲

You'll learn about directories in both UNIX and DOS in Chapter 3.

You can use the **PROMPT** command to change the DOS prompt to whatever characters you want. For instance, you can use the following command to change the prompt to the words *Hey You!*:

```
PROMPT "Hey You!"
```

As with DOS, the UNIX prompt can also be changed. And, surprisingly enough, the syntax is similar for both DOS and UNIX users. If you are using the Korn or Bourne shells, the following command would change the prompt to a greater-than symbol, the same as the symbol used in DOS:

```
$ PS1="> "
```

This command changes the string *$* to the string >, with a space after the > sign. (The space ensures that your commands don't abut the prompt— a move to cut down on potential confusion than anything else.)

You could enter this command at any point in your UNIX usage, or else you could enter this command in a special file that configures your system (a topic you'll cover later in this book).

If you're using the C shell, the following command changes a prompt:

```
% set prompt = "> "
```

Comparing the X Window System and Windows

The analogy can be extended to *Windows* and the X Window System. With *Windows*, you can launch programs and processes through **icons**, a small picture that represents a program in some manner. Figure 2.5 shows a typical *Windows* screen.

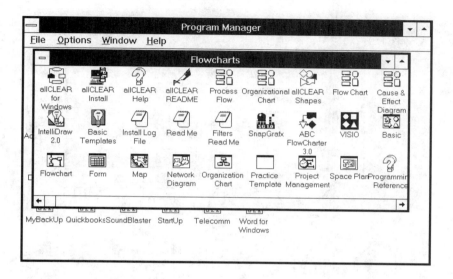

FIGURE 2.5 A typical Windows setup.

You'll notice that the Program Manager window contains a window labeled Flowcharts. In turn, this window contains a whole slew of icons, which represent programs and actions associated with those programs.

The same thing is true of a typical X Window System installation, as icons are used to represent programs and applications. Figure 2.6 shows the UnixWare (a version of UNIX for PCs) version of the X Window System running in OSF/Motif mode.

In this instance, several applications are running at the same time. Most are fairly standard in the X Window System world: ·

▲　**Xlogo** displays the logo for the X Window System. It is used most often at trade shows to tell unsuspecting observers that the X Window System is indeed running on a display.

▲　**Xeyes** features eyeballs that follow the cursor around the screen. This application loses its novelty factor after about 20 seconds, when you realize what an *immense* waste of computing power **xeyes** really is.

▲ **Xclock** displays a clock on the screen.

FIGURE 2.6 The X Window System and OSF/Motif running on UnixWare.

The UnixWare desktop also uses icons to represent programs and actions, as you can see in the window labeled *UnixWare Desktop— kevin*. Folders, meanwhile, contain other icons, organized around groups. To open a folder or access an icon, you double-click with the mouse—the same action used under *Windows*.

The similarity can be extended to how *Windows* and the X Window System allow direct commands to the operating system. Both allow you to create a direct window to the operating system. In the case of *Windows*, the MS-DOS Prompt icon in the Main program group opens up a window that contains a familiar DOS prompt, as shown in Figure 2.7.

In this instance, the window thinks that it is the only program running on the computer, just like a DOS program assumes that it is the only program running on the computer. In this window, you can run any DOS command from the prompt, as well as launch any program from the prompt.

In the X Window System world, the equivalent is the **xterm** program.

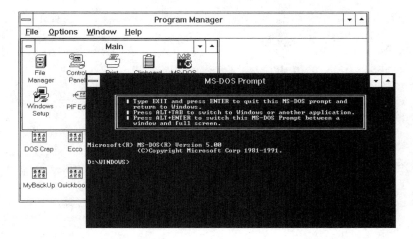

FIGURE 2.7 Windows with a DOS prompt.

By now, you should be very familiar with **xterm**—many of the illustrations in this chapter and Chapter 1 have shown **xterm** running under various window managers.

Xterm is a terminal emulator; as far as the program is concerned, it's the equivalent of a dumb terminal connected to a UNIX server. Some versions of the X Window System are set up to automatically launch an **xterm** or two whenever you start the X Window System.

This is technical

You should note that **xterm** and the DOS prompt aren't an exact analogy. With **xterm**, you run a command line, which launches an application running in its *own* window— the **xterm** window remains on the screen, although it doesn't accept input, and by and large, the only purpose it serves is to run the UNIX application. Conversely, the

DOS prompt acts as its own PC: When you start a program from the prompt, the program then becomes the only thing running in the window. No other windows are formed when you run an application in the DOS-prompt window.

There are some other similarities between *Windows* and the X Window System. Both use a **pointer** or **cursor** as a tool for moving about the screen. In *Windows*, the pointer is usually an arrow. In the X Window System, the cursor depends on the window manager and the whims of the system administrator. Due to a unique design in X, cursors are drawn from a font file, much like letters and other characters. Therefore, any drawing can be used as a cursor, so long as it is presented as a font to the system. Some popular X Window System cursors include the Gumby cursor (featuring a Gumby caught in midwave) and the U.S.S. Enterprise (from *Star Trek* fame) cursor. The Gumby cursor is pictured in Figure 2.8.

In addition, both treat the issue of window **focus** the same. A window that is ready to accept commands is said to have the focus. (Obviously, there must be only one window that accepts input at a given time—otherwise, chaos would rule and you couldn't keep track of exactly where your commands are going.)

FIGURE 2.8 The Gumby cursor, larger than life.

How can you tell which window has the focus? That's simple—it's usually colored differently than the other windows on the screen, both in *Windows* and the X Window System. In the default *Windows* configuration, for instance, the window that is accepting input is the one with a blue border; other windows on the screen have a white border. A similar coloring scheme is used by most implementations of the X Window System.

There's a twist that you may run into in the X Window System world, however. An X Window System setup can be changed to a **focus follows pointer** arrangement. In this situation—which is the default in the **twm** window manager, for instance—the window directly underneath the pointer is the one that is accepting input. There are ways to change this in virtually every X Window System implementation; check with your system administrator for details.

During the course of this book, you'll often be told to check with your system administrator regarding what seem to be simplistic tasks. Many times, systems are configured for specific circumstances, and quite often there's no one way to make changes to a UNIX or X Window installation. In these cases, it's always best to go to your system administrator and have them make the changes. With a UNIX system, there's always the possibility that you can do some serious damage by wiping out an essential file.

Using the Mouse

On the surface, there's one big consistency between *Windows* and the X Window System: the reliance on the mouse to select items on the screen.

For the most part, in both X and *Windows*, the left mouse button is used to select an item, whether it be dragging an icon, double-clicking on an icon, or highlighting a section of text. However, this is where *Windows* and X depart. *Windows* assumes only that a mouse is used, and that the mouse has two buttons (not so coincidentally, the popular Microsoft Mouse has only two buttons). However, *Windows* applications are free to appropriate the right mouse button, and many do so; for instance, the popular word-processing package *Word for Windows 6.0* uses the right mouse button to pop up a menu of frequently used commands.

The X Window System, on the other hand, assumes that you have a three-button mouse, and quite often all three buttons are utilized to one degree or another. Under OSF/Motif and the Motif Window Manager (**mwm**), for instance, the left mouse button is used to select items and text. In addition, the right mouse button under **mwm** is used to call on the Root menu when the cursor is placed over the screen's background, which allows you to move windows and refresh the contents of the screen. When the cursor is placed over an application, however, the actions associated with the right mouse button may differ. For instance, when you're working with an **xterm** window, a click on the right mouse button will bring up a menu of commands specific to **xterm**, covering such routine tasks as copying and pasting text.

Because the X Window System relies so heavily on specific buttons, it features several tools that allow you to change which mouse buttons do what; for instance, many left-handed users find it easier to switch the left mouse button to the right, making it more comfortable for selecting items on the screen. A popular tool is called **xmodmap**, and it ships with every version of the X Window System. The location of this program on your system may vary; see your system administrator about running this program and changing your mouse-button configuration.

Specific Mouse Actions

For most basic tasks, however, the mouse is used similarly in *Windows* and the X Window System.

▲   To make a window the active window, you move the pointer over the desired window and then click with the left mouse button.

▲   To move a window, you move the pointer over a window's titlebar and press on the left mouse button while dragging the window around the screen. (Some window managers go a step further and display the coordinates of the window on the screen as you drag the window around.)

▲   To resize a window, you place the cursor on the edge of the window, where it will change shape (with *Windows*, a two-ended arrow; with the X Window System, a corner). At this point, you drag the side of the window to the new size.

In Chapter 1, you were exposed to other similarities between a *Windows* window and an X Window System window—similarities that have mouse usage in common, such as the Maximize and Minimize buttons.

This Chapter in Review

▲   Though there are many differences under the hood when comparing UNIX and DOS, there are many similarities when it comes to issuing orders to the system.

▲   Both operating systems rely on commands to directly instruct the system what to do.

▲   Both operating systems allow commands to be modified by the addition of special characters, known as switches in DOS and options in UNIX.

▲   Both operating systems use prompts to tell you that the system is ready and awaiting your next command.

▲   Both operating systems call a combination of a command and its modifier a command line, which is entered at a prompt.

▲   The commands for listing the contents of a directory differ in the two operating systems. With DOS, the command is **DIR**. With UNIX, the command is **ls**.

▲   The similarities between UNIX and DOS can be extended to *Windows* and the X Window System.

▲   Both X and *Windows* use windows and icons to organize information on the screen.

▲   Both X and *Windows* use a mouse cursor or pointer to manipulate the windows on the screen—moving them, resizing them, or closing them.

▲   The X Window System treats mouse buttons differently, however, in assuming that every user will have access to three buttons. *Windows*, on the other hand, assumes that there are only two buttons on the mouse—and rarely is the second mouse button ever used by applications.

▪ CHAPTER THREE ▪
File and Directory Basics

M ost of your daily interaction with the UNIX operating system will center around the use of files and directories—tools that you'll use to store information. Topics in this chapter include:

- ▲   What a file is, and why it is important
- ▲   File basics and file types
- ▲   File and directory names
- ▲   The home directory and storing your work
- ▲   Rules when naming files
- ▲   Listing files with further permutations of the **ls** command
- ▲   File permissions in UNIX
- ▲   The current directory, and changing it
- ▲   Listing the current directory with the **pwd** command
- ▲   Absolute and relative pathnames
- ▲   Setting file permissions with the **chmod** command
- ▲   Moving through the directory tree with the **cd** command

What is a File, and Why is It Important?

Your honeymoon with the UNIX operating system is about to end. The first two chapters of this book stressed the similarities between UNIX and DOS as a way to ease your transition to a more complex operating system. Now comes your first exposure to the areas where UNIX and DOS seem to be very similar on the surface: files and directories. After all, both UNIX and DOS use files and directories as a way to store information, so there must be a great many similarities between them, right? In some ways, yes; but in more important ways, no.

The similarities have to do with the philosophical differences between the two operating systems. From the beginning, DOS was designed to serve the needs of a single user, while UNIX was designed from the start to serve many users scattered within the network. As a result, DOS contains few safeguards for protecting files from unwanted readers, while a huge portion of how UNIX deals with files has to do with who can read them.

This chapter will cover how both UNIX and DOS deal with files, and how UNIX deviates sharply in certain situations.

Starting On the Ground Level

A **file** is the mechanism for storing information on DOS and UNIX systems. Indeed, a great deal of what an operating system does centers around the usage and management of files. The instructions that make up the operating system are contained in a score of files. The information that you type in the system, such as letters and memos, are stored in files. Information about the operating system itself is stored in files.

Everything connected with DOS and UNIX can be traced to a file. When you use a command, you're actually calling upon a file, which contains instructions that are transmitted to the computer. When you want to print a letter, you call upon printer information contained in a file to make sure the letter is printed. When you want to run a program, you use a file containing the program's information.

With UNIX, there's a lot more emphasis placed on files, due to the way UNIX uses files to represent portions of the computer system. In fact, just about *everything* in UNIX is a file. When you print a file in DOS, for instance, you use a command and an option that specifies what computer hardware is to be used in printing the file. With UNIX, however, printing a file means specifying a file on the command line that actually carries out the work of printing the file. DOS users can pretty much assume that a local port can be used to print a file, but UNIX users can never assume the hardware.

Much of the discussion about files and directories in this chapter will deal with the issue in a general manner. Your specific hardware configurations—on both UNIX and DOS systems—may differ.

A file is represented by a **filename** on both DOS and UNIX systems. The filename tells the operating system where to look for information on the computer system's disk storage; the operating system takes this information and collects the information in a way that you can use.

This is technical

If you could actually view the contents of a hard disk directly, you'd see a bunch of symbols making little sense to you. On that level, the contents of a file are represented in **bits**. Because it would be silly for anyone to expect you to keep track of the 1,048,576 characters in a one-megabyte file, an operating system assigns a filename to the raw lump of data.

A file can be created directly by the operating system, or else it can be created by an application. The resulting file can contain pretty much anything an application wants it to contain. UNIX database managers, like *Oracle* and *Sybase*, create files with specially formatted data, as do page-layout programs like *FrameMaker*, which are available in both DOS (well, *Windows* actually) and UNIX versions. Again, you don't have to worry about these formats; the applications take care of this.

You've already seen files in action in Chapter 2, when the DOS **DIR** command and the UNIX **ls** command were used to list the files in a given directory. A typical result from the DOS **DIR** command is shown in Figure 3.1.

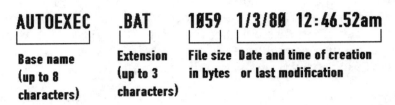

FIGURE 3.1 A parsed **DOS DIR** listing.

There are a few limitations to DOS filenames, as illuminated by Figure 3.1. A DOS filename is divided into two parts: the base name and the extension, which are separated by a period (.). The base name is limited to eight characters, while the extension is limited to up to three characters.

With such limitations, the emphasis in DOS is to provide highly descriptive filenames, which is usually accomplished through the use of specific extensions. The DOS community generally has agreed on a number of extension names common to specific types of files: *.BAT* denotes a batch file, *.COM* denotes a DOS command, *.EXE* denotes an executable file (that is, a file that can be run as a command), and *.TXT* denotes a text-only file. These are not the only extensions that are common in DOS—but since this is a UNIX book, we won't spend a lot more time on them.

By contrast, there is a lot more flexibility when it comes to filenames in UNIX. For starters, UNIX filenames can be up to 14 characters long. (Some versions of UNIX allow filenames of more than 14 characters, but this is by and large a false promise—the operating system recognizes only the first 14 characters anyway on most UNIX systems.) There's no need for a period to divide portions of the filename, though interestingly enough UNIX users have stolen a page from DOS users and informally adopted extensions even when they are not necessary. For instance, many C programmers use a suffix of *.c* to denote a source-code file, even though UNIX doesn't require the use of the period.

▼

File Rules

Still, there are a few rules to follow when you're naming files in UNIX—rules that differ from DOS.

▲   **A filename can be up to 14 characters long, generally speaking.** This isn't true across the board—the newest implementation of UNIX, System V Release 4, allows for unlimited lengths, though under the hood only the first 14 characters are acknowledged anyway—but it's still a good rule to follow, even if your specific system allows for more than 14 characters. Why? Because you'll often probably be typing filename into your system, and long filenames are a pain to type, as well as being more prone to causing errors on your part. In addition, the system recognizes only the 14 characters of the filename, anyway.

▲   **You must be specific about the case of the letters in the filename.** In UNIX, the following three filenames would be considered different files:

you
YOU
You

By contrast, it doesn't matter what case you use when you enter a DOS filename. In the end, the system will change every filename to uppercase anyway, when it displays the filename.

Very often, UNIX beginners are very frustrated when they know they are typing in the correct filename, only to discover that the system is denying access to the files because the case of a few letters was incorrect.

▲   **A filename is one word, with no spaces between.** UNIX uses spaces on a command line to break down the line into logical segments. Because of this, a filename can only be one word, without any spaces within the filename, the same as DOS. (By contrast, the Macintosh operating system allows spaces in filenames.) For instance, the following filename would be rejected by both DOS and UNIX:

```
my report
```

That's a shame, since most of us learned to anticipate spaces between words when we learned to read—*my report* is definitely a lot easier to pick out of a list than is *myreport*. Because spaces help us pick filenames out of lists, the UNIX community responded to the problem by inserting the underscore (_) character between words. To the eye, there's a space between the words. To the system, there's a character between the two portions of a single word:

```
my_reprt
```

This filename would be valid in both UNIX and DOS.

▲ **Not all keyboard characters can be used in a filename**. This is a matter of convention, not due to a limitation imposed by UNIX. (On a large system, you'll probably cause some problems if you use these characters. So don't.) DOS, on the other hand, allows most of these characters to be used in filenames. The frowned-upon UNIX characters are:

```
! @ # $ % ^ & ( ) [ ] ' " ? \ | ; < > 1` + - * /
```

▲ **You can place a period anywhere in the filename**. DOS requires that a filename be limited to eight characters, with up to three characters in the extension. The period (.) designated the end of the base name in a DOS filename. However, in UNIX, the period could appear anywhere in the filename. The following filename is valid in UNIX, but would cause a DOS system to choke:

```
1994.reports
```

More About the ls Command

In Chapter 2, you saw the **ls** command used in some pretty limited circumstances.

Depending on the options you use, you can divine quite a bit of information from the ls command. For instance, you can use the *–a* option to list *all* of the commands in the current directory, as shown in Figure 3.2.

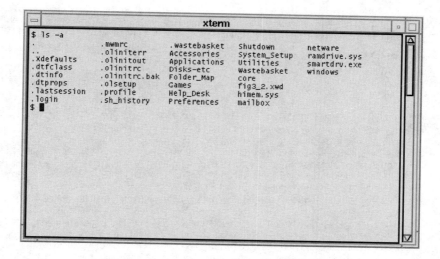

FIGURE 3.2 Using the ls command with the –a option.

As you saw in Chapter 2, the *–a* option lists all of the files in the current directory, including hidden files. There's no secret as to the identity of these files, so don't feel like there's some hidden information lurking within the system. Hidden files generally contain information specific to your UNIX usage and are thus important in the larger scheme of things. Hidden files are so called because they can't be seen by normal file-management tools (like the **ls** command with no options or any option other than the *–a* option) unless you explicitly look for them. Any file beginning with a period (**.**) is considered to be hidden by the UNIX operating system. You could create a file that began with a period and the system would consider it to be a hidden file. Still, you have access to these files, and by changing these files, you can change the way you use UNIX.

▼

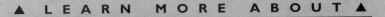

You will learn more about changing UNIX in Chapter 5.

To return information on a specific file or directory, type the name of the file or directory after the **ls** command:

```
$ ls data
data
```

If the file or directory in question was not contained in the current directory, you'd receive an error message like the following:

```
$ ls god
UX:ls: ERROR: Cannot access god: No such file or directory
```

So far, the **ls** command has not differentiated between files and directories. To do so, use the –*F* option:

```
$ ls -F
Accessories/    Folder_Map@  Preferences/   Utilities/
Applications/   Games/       Shutdown@      Wastebasket@
Disks-etc/      Help_Desk@   System_Setup/  core
```

Unless you tell it otherwise, the **ls** command will organize listings in a columnar fashion, with order descending through a column and then starting again on the next column. To sort entries *across* the screen in alphabetical order, use the –*x* option:

```
$ ls -x
Accessories   Applications  Disks-etc   Folder_Map
Help_Desk     Preferences   Shutdown    System_Setup
Wastebasket   core          data        mailbox
```

You can also combine options. For instance, you could apply both the –*x* and the –*F* options simultaneously:

```
$ ls -xF
Accessories/   Applications/  Disks-etc/   Folder_Map@
Help_Desk@     Preferences/   Shutdown@    System_Setup/
Wastebasket@   core           data         mailbox/
```

If you want to separate entries with commas instead of spaces, use the –*m* option:

▼

▼

```
$ ls -m
Accessories, Applications, Disks-etc, Folder_Map, Games,
Help_Desk, Preferences, Shutdown, System_Setup, Utilities,
Wastebasket, core, data, mailbox, netware
```

To return the contents of a directory in reverse order, use the *–r* option:

```
$ ls -r
netware    core         System_Setup   Help_Desk   Disks-etc
mailbox    Wastebasket  Shutdown       Games       Applications
data       Utilities    Preferences    Folder_Map  Accessories
```

To list the entries recursively—that is, to list the contents of the directories—use the *–R* option:

```
$ ls -R
./Accessories:
Calculator  Clock  Mail  Terminal  Text_Editor

./Applications:
DOS  Fingertip_Lib  Win  Win_Setup

./Disks-etc:
Disk_A  Disk_B  cdrom1

./Games:
Puzzle  Xtetris

./Preferences:
Backdrop_Library  Icons     Miscellaneous  Startup_Items
Color             Keyboard  Mouse
Desktop           Locale    ScreenLock

./Preferences/Backdrop_Library:
Backdrop_Items  aztec.gif  owl.gif  tallship.gif

./Preferences/Backdrop_Library/Backdrop_Items:

./Preferences/Startup_Items:
ScreenLock
```

```
./System_Setup:
Appl-n_Setup   Font_Setup      MHS_Setup
Dialup_Setup   Icon_Setup      NetWare_Setup
Extra_Admin    Install_Server  Password_Setup

./Utilities:
Backup-Restore  System_Status  UUCP_Inbox
NetWare_Access  Task_Scheduler

./mailbox:
```

As you can tell by the use of the *–R* option, there's the potential to generate a ton of information by using the **ls** command. Indeed, UNIX maintains a lot of information about each file—much more than the limited information you've generated so far. If you want to actually *see* all of this information—and there are definitely times where that is appropriate, as you'll see during a discussion of file permissions—use the *–l* (for *long*) option:

```
$ ls -l

total 2060
drwxr-xr-x  2 kevin   other      1024 Apr 29 21:23 Accessories
drwxr-xr-x  2 kevin   other      1024 Apr 29 21:23 Applications
drwxr-xr-x  2 kevin   other        96 May  1 10:23 Disks-etc
lrwxrwxrwx  1 kevin   other        25 Apr 29 21:23 Folder_Map
drwxr-xr-x  2 kevin   other        96 Apr 29 21:23 Games
lrwxrwxrwx  1 kevin   other        24 Apr 29 21:23 Help_Desk
drwxr-xr-x  4 kevin   othe       1024 Apr 29 21:23 Preferences
lrwxrwxrwx  1 kevin   other        23 Apr 29 21:23 Shutdown
drwxr-xr-x  2 kevin   other      1024 Apr 29 21:23 System_Setup
drwxr-xr-x  2 kevin   other      1024 Apr 29 21:23 Utilities
lrwxrwxrwx  1 kevin   other        28 Apr 29 21:23 Wastebasket
-rw-r--r--  1 kevin   other   1048576 Apr 30 11:50 core
-rw-r--r--  1 kevin   other       144 May  1 10:30 data
drwxr-x---  2 kevin   other        96 Apr 29 21:23 mailbox
lrwxrwxrwx  1 kevin   other         9 Apr 29 21:23 netware
```

The most common way to get a lot of information from the **ls** command is through the use of the *–l* option, which works roughly the same as the DOS **DIR** command. A typical result of the **ls –l** command line is shown in Figure 3.3.

As you can tell, this command line returns a lot of information—probably a lot more information than you'll ever need. However, a breakdown of exactly what each column means should illuminate a great deal about UNIX filenames.

Don't be so quick to use the *–l* option by itself, unless you're working on a smaller UNIX system. If you're working on a larger filesystem containing thousands and thousands of files, you may want to consider redirecting the output of the **ls** command to a file. Later in this chapter you'll learn about redirection, and one of the examples will involve the **ls** command.

```
┌─────────────────────────── xterm ───────────────────────────┐
│ $ ls -l                                                      │
│ total 2352                                                   │
│ drwxr-xr-x   2 kevin     other      1024 Apr 29 21:23 Accessories │
│ drwxr-xr-x   2 kevin     other      1024 Apr 29 21:23 Applications │
│ drwxr-xr-x   2 kevin     other        96 Jul  4 19:28 Disks-etc │
│ lrwxrwxrwx   1 kevin     other        25 Apr 29 21:23 Folder_Map -> /usr/X/de │
│ op/Folder_Map                                                │
│ drwxr-xr-x   2 kevin     other        96 Apr 29 21:23 Games    │
│ lrwxrwxrwx   1 kevin     other        24 Apr 29 21:23 Help_Desk -> /usr/X/des │
│ p/Help_Desk                                                  │
│ drwxr-xr-x   4 kevin     other      1024 Apr 29 21:23 Preferences │
│ lrwxrwxrwx   1 kevin     other        23 Apr 29 21:23 Shutdown -> /usr/X/desk │
│ /shutdown                                                    │
│ drwxr-xr-x   2 kevin     other      1024 Apr 29 21:23 System_Setup │
│ drwxr-xr-x   2 kevin     other      1024 Apr 29 21:23 Utilities │
│ lrwxrwxrwx   1 kevin     other        28 Apr 29 21:23 Wastebasket -> /usr/X/d │
│ top/dtwastebasket                                            │
│ -rw-r--r--   1 kevin     other   1048576 May  1 10:55 core    │
│ -rw-r--r--   1 kevin     other     83195 Jul  4 19:31 fig3_2.xwd │
│ -rw-r--r--   1 kevin     other     13824 Mar 10  1992 himem.sys │
│ drwxr-x---   2 kevin     other        96 Apr 29 21:23 mailbox  │
│ lrwxrwxrwx   1 kevin     other         9 Apr 29 21:23 netware -> /.NetWare │
│ -rw-r--r--   1 kevin     other      5873 Mar 10  1992 ramdrive.sys │
│ -rw-r--r--   1 kevin     other     43609 Mar 10  1992 smartdrv.exe │
│ drwxr-xr-x   3 kevin     other      2048 May 12 10:33 windows  │
│ $ ▮                                                          │
└─────────────────────────────────────────────────────────────┘
```

FIGURE 3.3 Using the ls command with the *–l* option.

The listing begins with a summary of the disk space (2352) used by the directory, as measured in blocks. (A block is usually 512 bytes, but this isn't a uniform measure across UNIXdom.) By looking at a specific line in the listing:

```
drwxr-xr-x   2 kevin  other   1024 Apr 29 21:23 Accessories
```

you can see exactly what information is returned by the **ls –l** command line. And by breaking down this line in reverse order (that is, right to left), the information associated with files should be made clearer.

The first column in our right-to-left explanation contains the files and directories in alphabetical order—in this case, `Accessories`. Because UNIX uses a ASCII-based alphabetization scheme, all of the uppercase letters appear at the beginning of a listing, followed by the lowercase letters. In such a listing, a file named **Zebra** would be alphabetized before a file named **alphabet**, because of the uppercase *Z* and the lowercase *a*.

Don't worry—you won't need to remember this explanation at any point in your UNIX usage.

In this case, **Accessories** is actually a directory, not a file. The **ls** doesn't distinguish between files and directories, unless you explicitly tell it to. But we're getting ahead of ourselves here—you'll learn more about directories later in this chapter.

The second and third columns (Apr 29 21:23) list the date and time the file was created or last changed.

The fourth column (1024) records the size of the file, or the amount of disk space it occupies, in bytes.

This is technical

Bits, Bytes, Kilobytes, and Megabytes

The computer world doesn't measure things in the same manner as the rest of the world. Take, for example, the rather confusing measures of file sizes—bits, bytes, kilobytes, and megabytes. A bit is the most basic measurement found in computing and is either 0 or 1 for a simple reason: The computer, on a base level, sees everything on an either–or basis. However, you'll never work with individual bits during the course of your computing experience. The smallest measure that you'll need to note is a byte (pronounced *bite*), which is eight contiguous bits and essentially a single character—the letter *a*, for example, is represented by a single byte. The next measurement is the kilobyte (K), and above that is the megabyte (MB). However, explaining these measurements is not as simple a matter as you'd think.

In many of the files listed when using the –*l* option (and as shown in Figure 3.3), the size of the file is returned as 1,024. That's a magical number in the computer world, as 1,024 bytes equals a kilobyte. This is not a mistake: Because computers process binary information, measurements like kilobytes and megabytes (and gigabytes and terabytes, if you're working with *very* large filesystems) are rendered in powers of 2. Therefore, 2^{10} equals 1,024 (which gives us a kilobyte) and 2^{20} equals 1,048,576 (which gives us a megabyte). The use of *kilo* and *mega* in this situation is misleading, since their usage has nothing to do with metrics.

And, to be honest, there are very few instances in which you'll need to know that a kilobyte is precisely 1,024 bytes, as opposed to around 1,000 bytes. However, it does help explain the recurring instance of 1,024 bytes: Many applications create files with a minimum size of 1 kilobyte—and when this measurement is translated to bytes, you end up with the magical 1,024.

The fifth column lists the group that the file belongs to.

▲ L E A R N   M O R E   A B O U T ▲

Groups will be discussed later in this chapter, so don't worry about them at the moment.

The sixth column lists the owner of the file. If you owned the file, your login name or username (which you will learn about in Chapter 4) would be listed here. (If you create a file, you are assumed to **own** that file.)

The seventh column is the link count, which lists how many files are symbolically linked to the file, or, in the case of directories, how many subdirectories are contained within plus two—one for the directory itself, and one for the parent directory. The minimum number for a directory is two (unless you have a **root** directory with no subdirectories—a highly unlikely occurrence), and that's exactly what we have in our example listing.

The final column—or, rather, the first column when reading left to right—contains what looks like a chaotic set of characters (`-drwxr-xr-x`). However, armed with knowledge, we can summon forth order from the chaos and parse the confusing string of characters, as shown in Figure 3.4.

This contents of this column, `drwxr-xr-x`, is actually four separate sections. The first character represents the file type—a concept covered in a later section, "File Types."

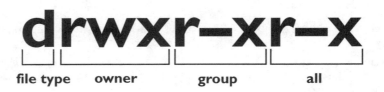

FIGURE 3.4 Parsed **UNIX** file permissions.

▲ L E A R N   M O R E   A B O U T ▲

For most of your computing needs, you'll only need to worry about directories (d), links (l), and ordinary files (–), which will all be explained later in this chapter.

Applying this information to our listing, we can see that the **Accessories** file is actually a directory. For the purposes of this discussion, this fact is relatively meaningless. However, it will become important later in this chapter when the discussion shift to directories.

Permissions

One of the most difficult concepts for DOS users to grasp is the idea of **permissions** assigned to UNIX files and directories. As a multiuser operating system that must simultaneously serve the needs of a potentially large number of users, UNIX must also have safeguards to ensure that every user can keep some data private—or, in reality, semiprivate.

In DOS, a file is said to have **attributes**, which means files can be:

▲ **Read-only**, where the operating system can read the contents of the file, but cannot make changes to the file, delete the file, or move the file.

▲ **Read-write**, where the operating system can read the contents of the file, make changes to the file, and move the file.

▲ **Archived**, where the file has been backed up to an archive using the **BACKUP** or **MSBACKUP** commands.

▲ **Not archived**, where the file has not been backed up to an archive using the **BACKUP** or **MSBACKUP** commands.

▲ **Hidden**, which means that the most DOS commands won't know about the file's existence.

▲ **System**, which means the file is part of the operating system.

To be honest, most DOS users don't deal with attributes very much, so if this is a new topic for you, don't worry about it.

▼

How can you divine attributes in DOS? By using the **ATTRIB** command, as shown in Figure 3.5.

```
                          MS-DOS Prompt                        ▼ ▲

   ▪ Type EXIT and press ENTER to quit this MS-DOS prompt and
     return to Windows.
   ▪ Press ALT+TAB to switch to Windows or another application.
   ▪ Press ALT+ENTER to switch this MS-DOS Prompt between a
     window and full screen.


Microsoft(R) MS-DOS(R) Version 5.00
        (C)Copyright Microsoft Corp 1981-1991.

D:\WINDOWS>cd\kevin\books\unixdos

D:\KEVIN\BOOKS\UNIXDOS>attrib *.doc
     A          D:\KEVIN\BOOKS\UNIXDOS\CHAP1.DOC
     A          D:\KEVIN\BOOKS\UNIXDOS\STYLE.DOC
     A          D:\KEVIN\BOOKS\UNIXDOS\UNIXDOS.DOC
     A          D:\KEVIN\BOOKS\UNIXDOS\CHAP2.DOC
     A     H    D:\KEVIN\BOOKS\UNIXDOS\~$CHAP3.DOC
     A          D:\KEVIN\BOOKS\UNIXDOS\CHAP3.DOC

D:\KEVIN\BOOKS\UNIXDOS>
```

FIGURE 3.5 The DOS ATTRIB command in action.

As you can see from the figure, all of the files have an *A* next to them, which means that they have not yet been archived.

However, an additional file, **~$CHAP3.DOC**, has an *H* in its list of attributes. This says that the file is a hidden file. As a result, most DOS commands, such as **DIR**, can't "see" them, so to speak. (*Windows*, on the other hand, lists hidden files in most applications.)

In many ways, this is an academic discussion, as most users don't mess with a file's attributes, since most users are in situations where attributes are meaningless. The only time that attributes become important is on a network, where key files needed by the entire workgroup are made hidden or read-only.

▼

Knowing this makes an explanation of UNIX file permissions a little clearer. UNIX provides a basic level of security through permissions, which dictate who can do what to a file—no matter if the file is an actual file, a directory, or a program. There are three levels of permissions associated with files:

▲ **Read**, where you can read the file.

▲ **Write**, where you can change the file.

▲ **Execute**, where you can run the file as a program (provided it's an executable file, of course).

Permissions can be applied to the owner of the file—usually the user who created the file—the group that lays claim to the file, or everyone on the UNIX network.

Permissions differ slightly when it comes to directories:

▲ **Read**, where you can list the contents of the directory.

▲ **Write**, where you can make or delete files or subdirectories within the directory.

▲ **Execute**, where you make the directory your current directory using the **cd** command.

By applying these guidelines to the parsed permissions information contained in Figure 3.4 as well as to an example file listing, you can learn a lot about permissions and how they apply to directories. As you can see in Figure 3.4, the permissions can be divided into four distinct sections. The first section, which you've already covered, covers the file type—and you already know that the file is actually a directory.

The second portion of the listing concerns the permissions for the owner of the directory, *rwx*. You'll recall that the owner of this file is *kevin*, and as such the user *kevin* can read (*r*), write (*w*), and execute (*x*) the directory.

The third portion of the listing, *r–x*, concerns the permissions for the group named *other*. Members of this group can read (*r*) and execute the directory (*x*), but cannot write to the directory (–). Permissions are noted in an either–or fashion—a user can either read/write/execute a file or directory (*rwx*) or not (---).

The fourth portion of the listing, *r–x*, concerns the permissions for *all* users of the UNIX system. Anyone can read (*r*) and execute the directory (*x*), but no one else can write to the directory (–).

Using the same format, you can see how permissions relate to files—specifically, the **data** file originating from the usage of the **ls –l** command line:

```
-rw-r--r--    1 kevin     other        144 May   1 10:30 data
```

Here the permissions are slightly different than you saw with the **Accessories** directory. To begin with, the listing in the file-type section, –, shows that the file is an ordinary file. (The next section will go into file types.)

The second portion of the permissions section, *rw–*, indicates that the owner of the file can read (*r*) or write (*w*) the file, but not execute (–) the file. Why not? For one simple reason: The system knows that the file is an ordinary file and not an executable file—and you can't execute a file that's not executable.

The third portion of the section, *r––*, is similar: The members of the group *other* can read (*r*) the file, but cannot write to it or execute it (–). The same goes for the fourth portion of the section, *r––*, which concerns the permissions of all users of the system.

Why are permissions important? Because users on a UNIX filesystem tend to take permissions very seriously. Many important files have specific permissions that will protect them from malicious or careless users. Also, permissions can trip up *any* UNIX user, not just beginners. A personal aside here: During the writing of a previous book in this series, this author was having a ton of problems with a relatively simple command, until it was pointed out that the author didn't have permission to write to a particular directory. After this was discovered, the command worked just fine. There are really two points to this: Even experienced UNIX users can be tripped up by something as basic as permissions, and you shouldn't take anything for granted when working with a UNIX system.

Changing Permissions with chmod

In this section, the permissions were represented in **symbolic form**. UNIX, owning up to its reputation as a complex operating system, also represents permissions in **numeric form**, using numerals (as you might expect) to represent the permissions.

The numeric form is actually very convenient when you want to change the permissions using the **chmod** (*change mode*) command. However, be warned that the use of the **chmod** can be a complex endeavor (as you'll see by browsing through Tables 3.1 and 3.2), so it's best to wade through the following examples and try to match an example to any changes you may want to make.

TABLE 3.1 COMMAND REFERENCE FOR THE CHMOD COMMAND.

> **chmod** *option mode filename(s)*
>
> *Purpose*
>
> The **chmod** command changes the permissions on a file or directory. Only the owner of the file or a privileged user can change the mode of a file. There are two ways to change permissions: through symbolic or numeric form. The numeric form is used to set absolute permission values, while the symbolic form is used to set values relative to the current value.
>
> *Option*
>
> **–R** Recursively changes through subdirectories and files.

Suppose you want to change the permissions associated with a file named **kevin.report**. You want to make sure that you (the owner) can read, write, and execute the file, but you want the members of your group and the rest of the UNIX users to be able to read the file, but not execute the file or write to it.

The command line to accomplish this would be:

```
$ chmod 744 kevin.report
```

At first glance, this isn't going to make any sense to you. However, the numeral *744* refers to the new modes you want to set for the file **kevin.report**. The **mode** is an octal number in one of the formats listed in Table 3.2.

TABLE 3.2 MODES AND THEIR MEANINGS

Numeral	*Meaning*
400	Owner has read permission.
200	Owner has write permission.
100	Owner has execute permission.
040	Group has read permission.
020	Group has write permission.
010	Group has execute permission.
004	All users have read permission.
002	All users have write permission.
001	All users have execute permission.

To get the permissions that you want to change to with the **chmod** command, you add the numbers. For example, 423 means that you, the user, can read the file, users in your group can write the file, and the rest of the world can write and execute the file. (You usually need read permission to execute a file, however, so having execute permission without having read permission is pretty worthless.)

In the example command line earlier, the value of *744* comes from adding together the mode values in such a manner. The lowest possible value is 000—which means no one can read, write, or execute the file—while the highest possible value is 777, where everyone can read, write, and execute the file. Here's the exact arithmetic used to arrive at 744:

400   Owner has read permission.
200   Owner has write permission.

100 Owner has execute permission.

040 Group has read permission.

004 World has read permission.

———

744

The next time you would run an **ls** command (using the long form, of course) on the file **kevin.report**, the permissions would be set as:

`rwxr--r--`

You can also use the symbolic form to set permissions. However, there's a slight difference between working with numeric and symbolic forms: When you're working with numeric form, you're setting the permissions in an absolute fashion, but when you're working with the symbolic form, you're setting the permissions relative to the current permissions. A few examples should make this clear to you.

For example: You want to allow yourself, the owner of the file, to execute the file named **kevin**. The following command line accomplishes this:

`$ chmod u+x kevin`

The *u+x* portion of the command line changes the permissions in the following manner:

- ▲ *u* specifies that you want to change the permissions for user, or the owner of the file.
- ▲ + specifies that you want to add a permission to the current permissions.
- ▲ *x* specifies that the change should be applied to the ability to execute the file.

Similarly, you can use this method to remove permissions. The follow command line takes away the ability to execute the file **kevin** from the owner of the file:

`$ chmod u-x kevin`

The *u–x* portion of the command line changes the permissions in the following manner:

▲   *u* specifies that you want to change the permissions for user, or the owner of the file.

▲   – specifies that you want to remove a permission from the current permissions.

▲   *x* specifies that the change should be applied to the ability to execute the file.

You can also combine various permissions in the same command line, making sure that the settings are separated by a comma (with no spaces on either side of it). In addition, you can set permissions for more than one set of users in the same mode statement, as shown in the following:

```
$ chmod u+x,go-w file.report
```

This allows the owner of the file **file.report** to execute the file, while removing the permissions of the group and all other users to write to the file.

The various symbols used with the **chmod** command, such as *x* and *g*, are listed in Table 3.3.

TABLE 3.3 SYMBOLS USED WITH THE CHMOD COMMAND.

Symbol	*Meaning*
u	User (who actually owns the file).
g	Group.
o	Other.
all	All (this is the default).
+	Add a permission to the current permissions.
–	Remove a permission from the current permissions.
=	Assign an absolute permission irrespective of the current permission.
r	Read.
w	Write.
x	Execute.
l	Mandatory lock during access.

There's a lot more associated with permissions, but most of it is of interest to system administrators and programmers.

Reality Check: Security

Setting permissions on files is the most rudimentary form of security available on a UNIX system. Unfortunately, there's no such thing as *absolute* security when it comes to file permissions. Even if you set up a permission that allows no one else but the owner of the file to read or write the file, there's one user who isn't affected by these permissions— the **root** or **superuser** of the UNIX system, who is considered a privileged user and has access to pretty much the entire UNIX system. Your system administrator has access to superuser status. If you're storing extremely sensitive material in your UNIX files, it would be a good idea to discuss a more potent security setup with your system administrator.

File Types

As you were reviewing information about file permissions, there were several references to **file types**. There's nothing mysterious or incomprehensible about file types, but it's information that you're probably need often if you work a lot with UNIX files.

The idea behind file types is simple. When *Oracle* creates a file, the resulting file is a specific type of file. When you create a text file for electronic mail, the resulting file is a specific type of file. Similarly, a programmer creates another type of file that ends up as part of a program. In these cases, the three different users were creating three different file types.

In UNIX, there are four main file types:

1. Ordinary files
2. Directories
3. Special device files
4. Links

When will you need to know the difference between these files? Anytime you're working with files, essentially.

Knowing that a file is an executable file, as opposed to a data file, can be useful information when you're looking for a file and you're not quite sure of the name. In addition, the knowledge that a file is executable will also let you know what programs you have on your system.

UNIX uses a single letter to represent the various file types, and these letters are listed in Table 3.4.

TABLE 3.4 FILE TYPES LISTED WITH THE –l OPTION.

Character	File Type
–	Ordinary file
b	Special block file
c	Special character file
d	Directory
l	Link
p	Named pipe special file

Ordinary Files

This is an instance where the UNIX jargon actually matches the reality of the situation—an **ordinary file** is rather ordinary in several ways. Essentially, you can think of ordinary files as data files. When *Oracle* or *FrameMaker* create files, they create ordinary files to store the data. The specific meaning of an ordinary file becomes clearer when you review the specific types of ordinary files.

▲   **Text files** contain ASCII characters. The ASCII format is a lowest-common-denominator format, containing representations of regular letters and numerals. If you use a text editor to create a letter and save it as a file, the resulting file will be in the ASCII format.

ASCII was created as a format that could be read by virtually every type of computer. An ASCII file created by a
UNIX text editor can be read directly by a Windows or
Macintosh word processor. A text file contains only the
characters you see on the screen.

▲ **Data files** are more complicated than text files, for they
contain both the data and how the data is to look and act
within an application. For instance: Let's say you create a
page using *FrameMaker*, a popular UNIX desktop-publishing
program. You create the page, put a headline on the top,
and place text on the remainder of the page. The resulting
file will contain the text you see on the page, but it will also
contain more information about that page: How large the
letters are to be when the file is printed, what fonts the letters are, and other information about the layout of the page
(margins, columns, etc.).

The same would be true of files created by database-
management programs like *Oracle*. If you pull a record from
an *Oracle* database and display it on the screen, all you'll see
is the specifics of the entry, such as the name, address, and
other information. What you *won't* see is the formatting
information contained within the database, or the other
entries within the database that aren't displayed.

Why does this matter? A common problem for most
users—beginner or intermediate—is realizing that data files
contain information specific to an application. For instance,
if you tried to read the *Oracle* database information in
FrameMaker or another UNIX application, you'd get either
an error message or a screen full of gibberish. Similarly, a

text editor made to work only with ASCII characters would choke on a file created in *FrameMaker*. This application-specific information creates problems in other applications. So while it seems logical that information you typed into *Oracle* should be accessible in a text editor, it doesn't work that way.

▲ **Command text files** are like text files, but with one big difference: They are meant to be used by the UNIX system to perform specific actions. (They act a lot like DOS batch files.)

▲ **L E A R N   M O R E   A B O U T** ▲

These files are also known as shell scripts, and they'll be covered in Chapter 5.

▲ **Executable files** are programs created by programmers. If you try to read an executable file with *any* application, you'll generate more than a few error messages. There are quite a few executable files within UNIX—remember, UNIX commands are nothing more than executable files. You've already covered commands in Chapter 1.

Directories

Directories organize files. Directories contain all pertinent information about a file: its name, its permissions, the date it was created, its type, and more. (No, you haven't covered this information yet.) There's a lot to be covered when it comes to directories, which is why the second half of this chapter is devoted to a discussion of directories.

Special Device Files

Special device files contain information about the different physical parts of the UNIX system. For instance, the printer connected to your UNIX system is represented by a special device file, as is your terminal,

▼

your neighbor's terminal, and all of the other terminals connected to the UNIX system.

This allows changes to be made easily to the UNIX system. For instance: If your system administrator were to connect a nice laser printer to the UNIX system and replace that grungy old dot-matrix printer, the only change to the system would be the changing of the device file that represents the system's printer.

You won't need to use device files very often, so don't worry too much about them. Generally, device files are set up by the system administrator to be bulletproof to changes from users—you'll be able to read the file and use it, but not make changes to it. If you want to print a file, just worry about the specific commands for printing that file. not the process.

Links

Links are an ingenious aspect of the UNIX operating system, although you won't have to worry too much about linking files. Still, an explanation of links illuminates how UNIX systems work, and so you might gain a little insight from them.

Computer hardware is expensive, especially when you're talking about the hardware needed to support 50 or more users. Especially expensive are disk drives needed to store all the information generated by all of these users, as well as the disk space needed by the UNIX operating system itself.

Links are used in order to occupy as little disk space as possible. A link is another name for an existing file located elsewhere on the system. Very often, a file you use will be used by another user on the system, whether it be a UNIX program or company information. Instead of having two separate files taking up precious disk real estate, UNIX allows two or more users to share the file by creating links to the file, and changes made by either user are reflected in the one file.

The best way to show how links work is to actually create one. Let's say that the user named **kevin** wanted to share information with the user named **geisha**. The information is stored in the directory named **/users/kevin**, under the filename clients.

The goal is to link that file to the same filename in a directory named **/users/geisha**. This is done with the **ln** command, as in the following:

```
$ ln clients /users/geisha/clients
```

After this is done, there's only one actual file: **clients**, stored in the directory **/users/kevin**. However, to the naked eye, there will be two files named **clients**, one in the **/users/kevin** directory and one in the **/users/geisha** directory.

In this example, **clients** was used to name both files. However, there's nothing that says both files need to have the same name. Some UNIX gurus recommend adding **.link** to the end of the linked file, so that they links are easier to find using other UNIX commands.

Don't reverse the file order with this command, or you can inadvertently trash good files. Remember: *the first file is the original file*. The second file names the link. The link then points back to the original file.

The **ln** command is explained more fully in Table 3.5.

TABLE 3.5 COMMAND REFERENCE FOR THE LN COMMAND.

ln *options originalfile linkfile*
ln *options file(s) directory*

Purpose

The **ln** command links two or more files. In essence, this allows the same file to be accessed under different names. No matter how many names exist, there's still only one file.

The **ln** command will also create linked files with the same name in different directories.

With System V Release 4, the **ln** command can create symbolic links, which can occur across filesystems, and they're easier to keep track of with the **ls** command.

continued

▼

> ***Options***
>
> **–f** Force linking—that is, do not ask for confirmations.
>
> **–n** Do not overwrite an existing file. (Not available on all systems.)
>
> **–s** Create a symbolic link.

On older UNIX systems, the links had to occur between two files residing on the same filesystem. However, the newest version of UNIX includes **symbolic links**, which allows files from two different filesystems to be linked. Generally speaking, you won't need to worry about whether or not a link is symbolic.

Creating a symbolic is a matter of adding the *–s* option to the **ln** command. For instance, to create a link between your system and a file on a remote filesystem named *othersystem*, you'd use a command like the following:

```
$ ln -s /othersystem/users/geisha/clients clients.link
```

This creates a file named **clients.link** on your system, linked to the file on the remote filesystem.

Directories

Because everything in UNIX is represented by a file, it also stands to reason that a large UNIX system, used by hundreds of users, could contain tens of thousands of files. Obviously, there needs to be a way to organize this potentially humongous number of files, as well as to make sure that files containing sensitive data—such as payroll information—are seen only by the appropriate workers.

DOS and UNIX allows for **directories**, used to group files. A directory itself is only a file containing the name of other files (following the UNIX practice of making *everything* within the system a file). The system looks inside these files in order to find information about the file in question.

A directory can be likened to a drawer in a file cabinet. Inside of the drawer are several file folders. A directory is nothing more than a file that contains the filenames of other files.

This is Technical

Figuring out how UNIX organizes directories can be a complicated task for the beginner, as UNIX isn't very friendly when it comes to information about directories. To make things more difficult, DOS directories are set up differently than UNIX directories; the DOS directory structure must serve the needs of a single user, while the UNIX directory structure must serve the needs of several users. And while the directory system may be logical for a system administrator or computer scientist, this logic isn't apparent to the beginning user.

Take a look at Figure 3.6. This is a drawing that represents the hierarchy of a UNIX directory system.

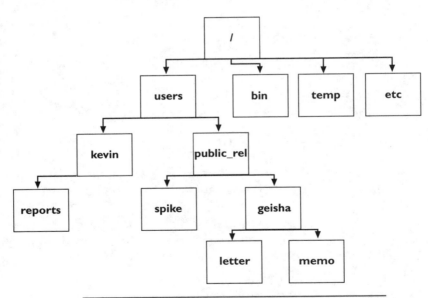

FIGURE 3.6 A portion of a UNIX directory structure.

Compare this to Figure 3.7, which shows a typical DOS file structure.

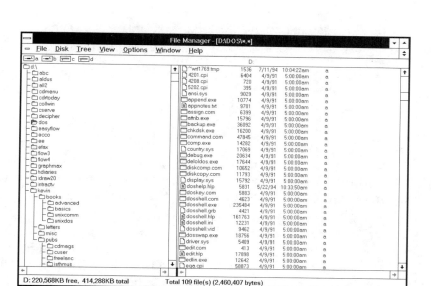

FIGURE 3.7 A portion of the DOS directory structure.

The big difference, obviously, is the differing depths found in the directory structures. DOS directory structures tend to a mile wide and an inch deep, while UNIX directory structures tend to be a foot wide and a mile deep. For instance, the most important DOS directories tend to be located at the top of the directory structure. An important directory like the DOS directory is contained immediately below the main directory, for instance.

A directory structure is often compared to a family tree. At the top of the family tree you have the directory that holds all other directories. In both UNIX and DOS parlance, this directory is the **root directory**. No directory can contain the root directory, and ultimately every other directory on both UNIX and DOS filesystems are contained within in the root directory.

The root directory isn't named like any other directory; instead, both UNIX and DOS use a single character to represent it. With DOS, the backslash character (\) is used to represent the root directory. With UNIX, the slash (/) represents the root directory.

For the UNIX beginner, this is a deceptively simple difference that will consistently be a pain in the butt. DOS users who first enter UNIX typically try to enter a filename in the DOS manner, forgetting that the UNIX method is the opposite. The difference is magnified because the same symbols are used to separate directories and subdirectories on a filename.

What's a subdirectory? Essentially, any directory that is contained within another directory. Technically speaking, *every* directory in a UNIX filesystem is a subdirectory, except for the root directory. But because of the multileveled way UNIX stores files, the use of the term subdirectory is used in reference to another directory.

Take a look at Figure 3.7. This representation of a filesystem uses lines to indicate the relationships between directories. For instance, the root directory (/) contains four subdirectories: **users**, **bin**, **temp**, and **etc**. Going down the family tree, you can see that users contains two additional directories, **kevin** and **public_rel**, while the directory **public_rel** contains the subdirectories **spike** and **geisha**, and so on. In this instance, it's said that **spike** is a subdirectory of the **public_rel** directory.

Looking at the directory tree from another direction, the directory **users** is said to be the **parent directory** of the **kevin** subdirectory.

Generally speaking, a UNIX directory tree won't be nearly as simple as this example. Since many UNIX filesystems must serve the needs of hundreds of users, there will be hundreds and hundreds of subdirectories on a typical UNIX installation. The root directory (/) usually contains at least six or seven subdirectories, and these subdirectories will hold tens or even hundreds of their own subdirectories. This is why wading through a UNIX filesystem is sometimes a very scary notion, particularly in a big company with lots of employees.

However, there is usually some semblance of order to a UNIX filesystem. Almost every UNIX system contains four or five basic directories contained directly within the root directory, such as **tmp**, **bin**, and **usr**. Even so, their usage is not universal; many UNIX systems don't have a directory named **users**, but may instead have a directory called **u** or **home**. Common subdirectories are listed in Table 3.6.

TABLE 3.6 COMMON UNIX DIRECTORIES.

Directory	Contents
bin	Most standard UNIX programs and utilities; the *bin* is short for binary.
dev	Device files, which represents different portions of the computer hardware.
etc	Miscellaneous files for the system administrator.
temp	Temporary files.
tmp	Temporary files.

Working with directories is not necessarily a simple task, especially if you are working on a large system with many, many directories. With the advent of graphics in the UNIX operating system, one of the handiest additions to many UNIX systems has been a file browser, which displays the UNIX file structure in a similar manner to the *Windows File Manager*. Your system may have a tool for displaying a UNIX file system, especially if your system features a graphical interface. For instance, UnixWare contains a handy utility for displaying files and directories, as shown in Figure 3.8.

UNIX file browsers tend to differ by vendor, so there's not really any one file browser to explain in a way that most UNIX users can use. However, much routine work with files and directories can be accomplished with the UNIX command line, and the rest of this chapter will focus on the command line.

The Current Directory

Like files and directories, a user must occupy a position on the directory tree. This is the same as DOS, so this isn't any news to you. The directory that you're "in" as you do your work is called your **current** directory (also referred to as your **working** directory). It is from this point in the UNIX filesystem that you perform your tasks.

How do you know what directory you are in? With DOS, you can use **DIR** to list of the contents of the current directory (which will include the name of the current directory), or else you can use the DOS **CD** command to list only the current directory. Both options are shown in Figure 3.9.

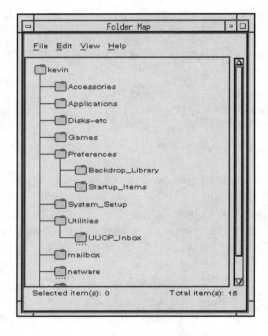

FIGURE 3.8 The UnixWare file browser.

Some users may use **CHDIR** instead of **CD** to change the current directory. Both DOS commands are appropriate.

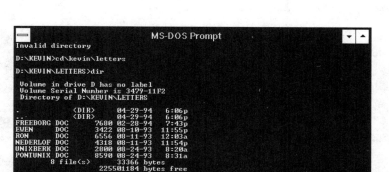

FIGURE 3.9 Listing the current directory.

With UNIX, the command to list the current directory is **pwd**, which is short for *print working directory*.

Figure 3.10 and Table 3.7 illustrate the **pwd** command.

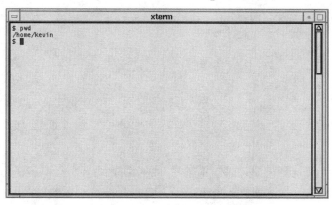

FIGURE 3.10 The pwd command in action.

TABLE 3.7 COMMAND REFERENCE FOR THE PWD COMMAND.

pwd
Purpose
The **pwd** command returns the current working directory.
Options
None.

A good DOS user knows that **CD** is used more to move around the filesystem than it is to list the current directory, however. Both DOS and UNIX use the same command—**CD** and **cd**, respectively—to change directories. And both commands are quite easy to use. In DOS, to change a directory, you use **CD** and then the name of the destination directory:

```
D:\WINDOWS> CD\KEVIN
D:\KEVIN> CD
D:\KEVIN
```

In this DOS example, the **CD** command was used to both change directories and list the current directory.

The UNIX command **cd** (short for *change* directory) also changes the current directory. It's a simple command, and its syntax is very simple:

```
cd directory
```

where *directory* is the name of the new current directory.

In DOS, you saw the following command used:

```
CD\KEVIN
```

Meanwhile, the following command is used in UNIX:

```
cd directory
```

This points to one huge difference between DOS and UNIX: In DOS, there's no need for a space between the portions of a command line. There was no need for a space between **CD** and the new directory. By contrast, the UNIX system will choke if you don't leave a space between the command and the input for the command. This small point *always* trips up UNIX beginners.

Table 3.8 lists the command reference.

TABLE 3.8 COMMAND REFERENCE FOR THE CD COMMAND.

cd *directory*

Purpose

The **cd** command changes the current directory to a new directory.

Options

None.

Before you learn how to use the **cd** command, you'll need to learn about pathnames—both absolute and relative. As a matter of fact, you'll learn a lot about the **cd** command as you learn about pathnames.

Absolute Pathnames

Every file occupies a specific place on the UNIX filesystem, as does every directory. (And so does every user, so to speak.) The exact way that UNIX uses to denote this place is a combination of file and directory names.

Let's go back to Figure 3.6, which showed a very small portion of a typical UNIX file structure. If you were to follow the lineage of the file **letter**, which you can find at the bottom of the tree structure, you'd see that it is contained in a series of directories, in a direct line to the root (/) directory. If you were to list this path, the result would be **/users/public_rel/geisha/letter**. This is how you determine a file's **absolute pathname**.

At first glance, an absolute pathname looks confusing—though less so for a DOS user who's worked with DOS files and directories. If you were to break apart the portions of an absolute pathname, you'd see that it makes sense:

▲   The root directory always begins an absolute pathname and is represented by the first slash (/).

▲ A move down the directory tree is represented by another slash (/).

▲ The first subdirectory of the root directory is **users**.

▲ The **public_rel** directory is a subdirectory of **users**, which in turn is a subdirectory of the root directory, represented by the leading slash (/).

▲ The **geisha** directory is a subdirectory of **public_rel**, which is a subdirectory of **users**, which in turn is a subdirectory of the root directory, represented by the leading slash (/).

▲ The **letter** file is contained in the **geisha** directory, which is a subdirectory of **public_rel**, which is a subdirectory of **users**, which in turn is a subdirectory of the root directory, represented by the leading slash (/).

You'll use this absolute pathname when you work with files outside your home directory. UNIX commands, such as the **ls** command that you've already seen in action, work on the current directory and files within it. If you want to use the **ls** command on a directory other than the current directory, your choices are to either change your current directory with the **cd** command or to specify the absolute pathname in conjunction with the **ls** command.

For instance, you may want to verify that the **memo** file exists by using the **ls** command. However, the **ls** command works only on the current directory unless you tell it otherwise, and it can be used to generate a listing for a single file. Putting these two nuggets of information together, you can then look for a single file in a directory other than your current directory. The resulting command line would look like this:

```
$ ls /users/public_rel/geisha/letter
/users/public_rel/geisha/letter
```

If the file were not found, the **ls** command would return that information, too:

```
$ ls /users/public_rel/geisha/letters
File not found
```

Relative Pathnames

Working with absolute pathnames is a big pain, however, especially on a UNIX system that can have many, many layers of nestled subdirectories. There's a handy tool not found within DOS, but is featured in UNIX, that will cut down on the potential amount of typing.

A **relative pathname** is just what the name implies—a pathname that's shortened in relationship to your present directory position. A good way to illustrate a relative pathname is to use an example. When you login a UNIX system, you're always placed in your home directory.

You don't need to know the larger ramifications of this act at the moment; you'll learn about logging in a system in the next chapter.

The best way to illustrate relative pathnames is to use an example, again using the directory structure showed in Figure 3.6.

Absolute filenames begin with a slash (/), indicating that the filename is relative to the root directory (/). With relative pathnames, you can specify a file or directory relative to your current position in the UNIX filesystem.

For instance: If your current directory is the **users** directory, the relative pathname to the **public_rel** directory is merely **public_rel**. To make **public_rel** your current directory, you'd use the following command line:

```
$ cd public_rel
```

Because there's no slash beginning the pathname, UNIX knows that the path is relative to the current directory—in other words, the pathnames start at the current directory, not the **root** directory.

Relative pathnames also work when moving up through the directory tree. UNIX, as well as DOS, uses two dots (**..**) as a shorthand for the directory above the current directory. You can use the dots to specify one move up the directory tree, again relative to the current directory (and again the same as DOS).

Again, using Figure 3.6 as an example: **spike** is your current directory, and you want to make **geisha** your current directory. Instead of typing out the cumbersome command line:

```
$ cd /users/public_rel/geisha
```

you can specify the **geisha** directory relative to your current directory:

```
$ cd ../geisha
```

This command tells the system to move up one level on the directory tree (as specified by **..**) and then to the subdirectory **geisha** (as specified by *geisha*).

UNIX doesn't care if you use absolute or relative pathnames. You can use both within command lines. The key is accuracy when using either method.

Reality Check: Using Relative Pathnames

A mistake many beginners make—as well as many more experienced users—is assuming that a relative filename can be used all the time. For instance, why not use the following command line to change the current directory to **geisha**, since it lists a relative pathname?

```
$ cd public_rel/geisha
```

If you tried this command line, you'd get an error message, saying that the **public_rel/geisha** directory was not found:

```
$ cd public_rel/geisha
UX:cd: ERROR: public_rel/geisha: Does not exist
```

Indeed, it doesn't exist—at least in the example directory tree shown in Figure 3.6. The above command line tells the UNIX system that you want to change your current directory to a *subdirectory* of the current directory—and **public_rel/geisha** is indeed not a subdirectory of the current directory. Always remember that when moving up and down the directory tree and using relative pathnames, you must use two dots (**..**) to move *up* the tree.

This Chapter in Review

▲ Everything within the UNIX operating system is a file. Most of your daily UNIX usage will involve files. Therefore, it's important for you to have a clear idea of how files function within UNIX.

▲ There are four main types of files within UNIX: ordinary, directories, special device files, and links.

▲ A directory structure is often compared to a family tree. At the top of the family tree is a directory called the **root** directory.

▲ Pathnames indicate the placement of files in the directory structure. Pathnames can be absolute—descending in a straight line from the **root** directory—or relative to the current directory.

▲ To view the contents of a directory, use the **ls** command. This lists all files and directories contained within a given directory. It will also return a lot of information about the specific files and directories, such as the permissions, the time the file was last changed, and the owner of the file.

▲ Permissions control who can do what to a file or directory. The owner of a file, a group, or all users can read a file, write to a file, and/or execute a file.

▲ Changing files permissions is accomplished through the use of the **chmod** command. However, changing file permissions is a tricky business, and before you change permissions, you may want to read through the **chmod** examples.

• CHAPTER FOUR •
Commands for Using Files and Directories

Knowing how to navigate through files and directories is one thing. Knowing what commands to use when working with those files and directories is an important advance in your UNIX education. Topics in this chapter include:

- ▲   Working with files and directories
- ▲   Using DOS wildcards
- ▲   Using UNIX wildcards
- ▲   Using wildcards in *Windows* and UNIX file managers
- ▲   Removing files with **rm**
- ▲   Copying files with **cp**
- ▲   Moving files with **mv**
- ▲   Renaming files in UNIX
- ▲   The dangers of erasing files in UNIX
- ▲   Creating directories with the **mkdir** command
- ▲   Removing directories with the **rm** and **rmdir** commands
- ▲   Copying entire directories, including any subdirectories

Working Directly With Files and Directories

Now that you've learned about files and directories, the next step in your UNIX education will center on actually using files and directories directly.

As you work through this chapter, you'll again be amazed by the similarities between DOS and UNIX. Indeed, many of the commands used for common tasks, such as creating a directory, are the same in both operating systems. And some very useful conventions in DOS, such as wildcards, also exist in UNIX.

This chapter will begin with a discussion of wildcards and then move to common DOS commands applying to files and directories that have analogues in UNIX.

Wildcards

If you've moved around a lot of files in DOS, you already know about **wildcards**, characters that are substituted for a character or group of characters when working with files. Both UNIX and DOS use wildcards. Although the two operating systems differ somewhat on the details, both tools are close enough in usage for any DOS user to make a successful transition to UNIX.

A short review of the DOS wildcard characters is in order.

DOS Wildcards

The most common DOS wildcard is the asterisk (*), which tells DOS to substitute any character or characters that appear in the place of the wildcard. For example, the command line shown in Figure 4.1 uses the asterisk wildcard in a search for all files ending with an extension of *TXT*.

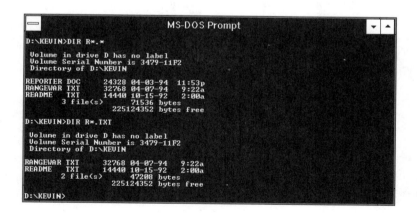

FIGURE 4.1 The DOS asterisk (*) wildcard in action.

Similarly, the DOS asterisk wildcard can be used as a substitute for part of a filename, as shown in Figure 4.2. In addition, you can use two wildcards in the same command line, one as part of the filename and one as part of the extension—an action also illustrated in Figure 4.2.

FIGURE 4.2 Other usages of the DOS asterisk (*) wildcard.

DOS wildcards—as well as UNIX wildcards, for that matter—can also apply to directories, as shown in Figure 4.3.

FIGURE 4.3 A wildcard listing both files and directories.

There is one annoying limitation to the DOS asterisk wildcard, however: Once a command line reaches the asterisk either in the filename or the extension, the remaining characters in the filename or the extension are ignored, an occurrence illustrated by Figure 4.4.

There is another DOS wildcard character, though it tends not to be widely used as the asterisk wildcard. If your needs are more precise than the asterisk wildcard offers—as shown in Figure 4.4—then there's always the question-mark (**?**) wildcard, which is a one-for-one substitute for a character. When you use it, DOS acknowledges the rest of the filename or the extension; with the asterisk wildcard, it stops.

The difference between the two is shown in Figure 4.5, which shows both the ***** and **?** asterisks in action. When using the asterisk wildcard, the command line returns every file beginning with the letter *p*. However, when there's a search done for every file beginning with *print* using the ? wildcard, only one file is returned—

PRINT.EXE—and the file named **PRINTER.SYS** is ignored. Why? Because a wildcard—whether it be an asterisk or a question mark—can also stand for nothing at all. But the question-mark wildcard stands for a *single* character, and in the case of the file **PRINTER.SYS**, there are *two* characters after the string *print*.

```
═════════════════════════ MS-DOS Prompt ═════════════ ▼ ▲

D:\KEVIN>dir S*E.*

 Volume in drive D has no label
 Volume Serial Number is 3479-11F2
 Directory of D:\KEVIN

STEVE        DOC     14336 01-21-94   3:24p
STEVE2       DOC     12288 02-03-94   9:12a
STEVE3       DOC     10240 02-09-94  10:54a
SYSTEM       INI      2475 07-07-94  11:43a
SETUP        EXE     61392 10-15-92   2:00a
        5 file(s)        100731 bytes
                      223928320 bytes free

D:\KEVIN>
```

FIGURE 4.4 An unfortunate limitation to the DOS asterisk wildcard.

```
═════════════════════════ MS-DOS Prompt ═════════════ ▼ ▲

D:\DOS>dir p*

 Volume in drive D has no label
 Volume Serial Number is 3479-11F2
 Directory of D:\DOS

PACKING  LST      2650 04-09-91   5:00a
PRINT    EXE     15656 04-09-91   5:00a
PRINTER  SYS     18804 04-09-91   5:00a
        3 file(s)        37110 bytes
                      222773248 bytes free

D:\DOS>dir print?

 Volume in drive D has no label
 Volume Serial Number is 3479-11F2
 Directory of D:\DOS

PRINT    EXE     15656 04-09-91   5:00a
        1 file(s)        15656 bytes
                      222773248 bytes free

D:\DOS>
```

FIGURE 4.5 The question-mark wildcard in action.

Windows and Wildcards

If you've worked a lot with the *Windows* File Manager, you probably already know that it allows you to use wildcards with most of its commands. A very common usage of wildcards within File Manager is shown in Figure 4.6.

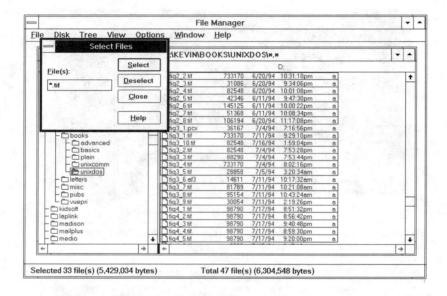

FIGURE 4.6 The asterisk wildcard and the Windows File Manager.

UNIX Wildcards

UNIX wildcards work very similarly to DOS wildcards; if you made it through the previous section with no problems, you'll have no problems either with UNIX wildcards.

There are three UNIX wildcards: *****, **?**, and **[...]**, as listed in Table 4.1. Each type will be covered in this section.

TABLE 4.1 UNIX WILDCARDS.

Wildcard	Meaning
*	A string of characters.
?	A single character.
[set]	Any character in a *series* of characters.
[!set]	Any character not in a *series* of characters.

The best way to explain UNIX wildcards is to show them in action. Let's start with a typical UNIX directory, as shown in Figure 4.7.

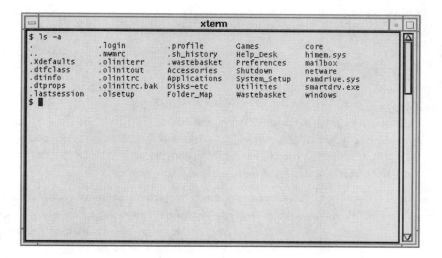

FIGURE 4.7 The contents of a typical UNIX directory.

The **ls –a** command lists all the files in the current directory, including hidden files. There are times when you'll want to list only a portion of the files in the directory. Or you may want to look for a specific file, but you can't remember the name of the file—just that it begins with a specific letter, such as the letter *a*. In this instance, you can use wildcards to hone your searching abilities.

An example: You know that the file you want begins with the letter *a*, but you don't know the rest of the filename. You can combine the asterisk (*****) wildcard with the **ls** command to list all files beginning with *a*:

```
$ ls a*
UX:ls: ERROR: Cannot access a*: No such file or directory
```

Gotcha! As you'll recall, case matters in UNIX. As you can see from the earlier listing of the current directory, there are no files or directories that begin with a lowercase *a*. Let's try the command with an upper-case *A*:

```
$ ls A*

Accessories:
Calculator    Clock    Mail    Terminal    Text_Editor

Applications:
DOS    Fingertip_Lib    Win    Win_Setup
```

This tells us that there are two directories beginning with *A* (**Accessories** and **Applications**). How do we know that they are directories? Because the **ls** command listed the subdirectories contained within the directories. However, there are no files in the current directory that begin with an *a*—uppercase or lowercase.

Because UNIX filenames are not subject to the same restrictions as a DOS filename—that is, an eight-character filename followed by a three-character extension—you don't need to worry about a period and an extension when working with wildcards. Within UNIX, a period is merely another character within the filename—not the designated separator between a filename and an extension.

It's clear, then, that your recollection is faulty regarding the filename. You think that the filename may begin with a *d*, and so you use the **ls** command in conjunction with the wildcard *****:

```
$ ls d*
data
```

This command shows that there is indeed a file beginning with the letter *d*: **data**.

 One important thing to remember when working with the asterisk (*) wildcard: It can also stand for nothing. The following command line and answer is perfectly valid within UNIX:

```
$ ls data*
data
```

Wildcards also work on hidden files if you're using the **ls** command. To generate a listing of hidden files (remember, hidden files begin with an period), use the command line shown in Figure 4.8.

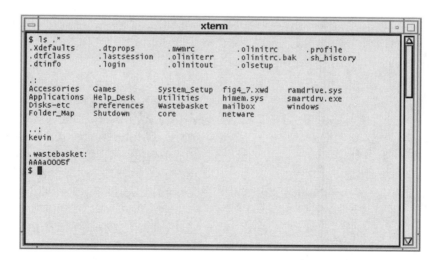

FIGURE 4.8 Using wildcards to find hidden files.

Why all the additional information? Remember: The current directory and the parent directory also begin with periods (. and ..). The contents of the current directory (.) are also listed, as well as the parent directory (..). When there's more than one file or directory that meets the criteria established by the command and the wildcard, the shell will return all such instances, as shown in the following command line:

```
$ ls .ol*
.oliniterr   .olinitout   .olinitrc   .olsetup
```

Because it's so flexible, the asterisk (*) wildcard will probably dominate your wildcard usage. However, there are other types of wildcards that you'll occasionally find useful.

The **?** wildcard works similarly to the asterisk (*) wildcard—the same as in DOS—except for one crucial difference: It matches *only* one character, instead of an unspecified number of characters. Here's an example of the **?** wildcard:

```
$ ls file.?
file.1   file.3   file.5   file.8
file.2   file.4   file.7   file.9
```

In this instance, the **ls** command would fail to return filenames with more than one character, such as **file.10** or **file.11**.

Finally, there's the **set** wildcard. This wildcard allows you to name one or more specific characters to match (such as *a*, *b*, and so on) as well as a range of possible characters (*a–z*, *1–10*). DOS users may find this wildcard unfamiliar, and to be honest, its usefulness is more limited than you may think—but hey, this is a complete guide to UNIX. The set wildcard gives you the greatest control over the characters you want to match with the wildcard, as it allows to you be the most specific.

A few examples should illustrate the set wildcard. To find files in the current directory that end in the letters *c* and *o* (common file suffixes used by programmers), you could use the following command line:

```
$ ls *.[co]
code.c   program.c   program.o
```

In this case, you asked for filenames where the beginning of the filename could be anything, as long as there was a period in the filename, followed by either a *c* or an *o*. To search for filenames that begin with *program* and end with either *c* or *o*, you'd use the following filename:

```
$ ls program.[co]
program.c   program.o
```

You can also use the set wildcard to specify a range of characters. For instance, the following command line lists the filenames beginning with *program* and ending with any letter between *a* and *f*:

```
$ ls program.[a-f]
```

As always, case counts in UNIX. The previous example would return **program.a**, **program.b**, and so on through **program.f**, but would not return **program.A**, **Program.a**, **PROGRAM.A**, or any variation where all the characters in the filename were not lowercase.

You can also specify characters *not* to be returned by the set wildcard, using an exclamation point (!). For instance, to specify all characters *except* for the letter *a*, you'd use the following command line:

```
$ ls program.[!a]
```

A fuller set of examples using the set wildcard is listed in Table 4.2.

TABLE 4.2 THE SET WILDCARDS IN ACTION.

Wildcard	Meaning
[xyz]	Matches *x*, *y*, or *z*.
[.-_]	Matches ., -, and _.
[a-f]	Matches *a*, *b*, and so on through *f*.
[a-z]	Matches any lowercase letter.
[A-D]	Matches *A*, *B*, *C*, and *D*.
[A-Z]	Matches any uppercase letter.
[a-zA-Z]	Matches any letter.
[!z-z]	Matches any character except lowercase letters (**ksh** shell only).

This is technical

There are some serious drawbacks to the set wildcards. For starters, don't assume that the use of ranges is necessarily accurate on your computer system. The computer *really* doesn't keep track of specific letters and numerals, but rather numerical representations of letters. Because of the different ways different computers keep track of these letters and numerals, the use of sets shouldn't assumed to be totally reliable. You don't need to know *why* this occurs—unless discussions of ASCII and EBCDIC really excite you—but you should be aware of this fact.

Wildcards and File Browsers

There's a wide range of file browsers in the UNIX world, but most support wildcards when working directly with files. The UnixWare file browser, complete with a wildcard in action, is shown in Figure 4.9.

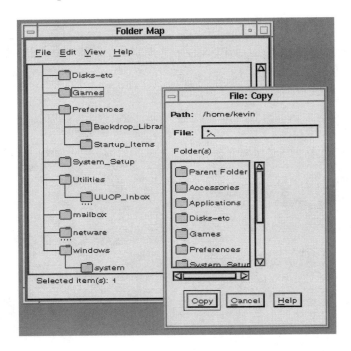

FIGURE 4.9 The UnixWare file browser and a wildcard.

A Short Summary of Wildcards

What should you gain from this section? The knowledge that wildcards in DOS and UNIX work *very* similarly. If you can work with a wildcard in DOS, you can certainly work with a wildcard in UNIX.

Working With Files

There are a lot of similarities between DOS and UNIX when it comes to working with directories, as you'll see in this section.

Copying and Moving Files

DOS uses the **COPY** command to copy files from one location on the directory tree to another. (The **COPY** command can also be used to join files into a single file, but this is infrequently utilized.) When you copy a file, the original file remains intact, while a copy is created in the destination location.

For instance: The following command line copies the file **REPORT**, currently located in the **KEVIN** directory, to the same name in the **GEISHA** directory:

```
C:\WINDOWS> COPY REPORT \GEISHA
```

If you want to give the copied file a new name, you can specify it on the command line:

```
C:\WINDOWS> COPY REPORT \GEISHA\REPORT.BAK
```

In UNIX, the similar command is called **cp** (which is short for copy). You would use it in the same exact manner: Specify the copy to be moved, then the destination:

```
$ cp report /geisha/report
```

Again, you can give the copied file a new name by specifying the new name as part of the destination:

```
$ cp report /users/geisha/report.bak
```

There's one crucial difference between the two commands. If you want to copy a file to a new location that already contains a file by the same name, DOS **COPY** will warn you that you are about to overwrite an existing file, and confirm that you indeed do want to overwrite the existing file. By contrast, **cp** doesn't tell you if your actions will end up overwriting an existing file. In the previous example, if a file named **report.bak** had already existed in the **/users/geisha** directory, the **cp** command would have overwritten the existing file without as much as a peep.

To avoid this danger, UNIX System V Release 4 users can use the *–i* option to the **cp** command, which will make sure that you do indeed want to overwrite the existing file:

```
$ cp -i report /users/geisha
cp:  overwrite report ?
```

If you want to overwrite the existing file, type **y**. If you do not want to overwrite the existing file, type **n**.

The DOS **COPY** and UNIX **cp** commands are summarized in Table 4.3.

TABLE 4.3 COMPARISON OF THE COPY AND CP COMMANDS.

COPY	cp
Purpose	
Creates a copy of a file in a new location on the computer system.	
Usage	
DIR *SOURCE DESTINATION SWITCHES*	cp *options sourcefile destinationfile*
	cp *options file1 directory*
	cp *options directory1 directory2*
	continued

Switches	Options
/A Tells **COPY** that the file is an ASCII file. (Used when combining files.)	**–i** Makes sure you don't overwrite existing file.
/B Tells **COPY** that the file is a binary file. (Used when combining files.)	**–p** Retains existing permissions. (Not available on all systems.
/V Verifies that a successful copy occurred.	**–r** Copies entire directory.

When it comes to moving files, UNIX goes a step beyond what is available in DOS. To move a file in DOS—that is, not leave the original file in the original location—you first need to copy the file and then delete the original:

```
C:\WINDOWS> COPY REPORT \GEISHA
      1 file(s) copied
C:\WINDOWS> DEL REPORT
C:\WINDOWS>
```

With UNIX, you can combine the two operations with a single command: **mv** (short for *move*). The following command line moves a file from the current directory to a new directory:

```
$ mv report /users/geisha
```

There's really not a lot to the **mv** command: Merely list the file to be moved, along with the new destination. If you want to move the file and retain the existing name, then just list the new directory. If you want to move the file and give it a new name, list it as part of the new directory:

```
$ mv report /users/geisha/report.bak
```

The **mv** command shares one trait with the **cp** command: It will not warn you when you rename a file to a name already in use. The old file will be wiped out, and the new file will be stored under the new name.

Like **cp**, newer versions of UNIX—specifically, System V Release 4—support the use of the *–i* option to prevent you from accidentally overwriting an existing file, as shown in the following command line:

```
$ mv -i report /users/geisha
cp:  overwrite report ?
```

If you want to overwrite **report**, type **y**. If you do not want to overwrite **report**, type **n**.

Other options to **mv** are listed in Table 4.4.

TABLE 4.4 COMMAND REFERENCE FOR THE MV COMMAND.

> **mv *options sources target***
>
> **Purpose**
>
> The **mv** command moves a file or multiple files into another directory or to a new name in the current directory.
>
> **Options**
>
> **–f**   Moves file without checking for confirmation in case of an overwrite.
>
> **–i**   Prompts users if action would overwrite an existing file. (Not available on all UNIX systems.)

Renaming Files

DOS users are accustomed to using the **REN** command for renaming file. For instance, the following command line renames the file **REPORT** to **REPORT.BAK**:

```
C:\ REN REPORT,REPORT.BAK
```

In UNIX, there's no analogue to the **REN** command (oddly enough, since UNIX folks love to create new commands at the drop of a hat).

▼

You must use the **mv** command to rename a file; instead of listing a destination, you list a new filename, as in the following command line:

```
$ mv report newfile
```

This leaves the file named **newfile** in the same directory.

Erasing Files

DOS users are probably all too familiar with the dreaded **DEL** command, which will delete a file or a group of files. To delete a file named **SUMMARY**, a DOS user would use the following command line:

```
C:\WINDOWS> DEL SUMMARY
```

The file will then be erased, with no feedback from the system. Experienced DOS users will also use the */p* switch when using the **DEL** command. This switches verifies that you indeed do want to erase the file:

```
C:\WINDOWS> DEL SUMMARY /P
    Are you sure (Y/N)?
```

If you want to erase the file, type **y**. If not, type **n**.

The **rm** command in UNIX works pretty much the same. You can use it to erase a specific file. By default, it doesn't check with you before it actually erases the file. A typical **rm** command line looks like the following:

```
$ rm summary
```

The UNIX **rm** also supports an option——*i*, which would be pretty familiar to you by now—that will verify whether or not you really do want the file erased:

```
$ rm -i summary
summary: ?
```

If you want to erase the file, type **y**. If not, type **n**.

However, **rm** also adds a few twists to the matter. As you know by now, UNIX has many safeguards that prevent users from doing damage to files that they do not own. The **rm** command, then, works only on files that you own. It will also allow you to remove the files if you have write permission *to the directory containing the file*, though not necessarily to the file itself.

The DOS **DEL** and the UNIX **rm** commands are summarized in Table 4.5.

TABLE 4.5 COMPARISON OF THE DEL AND RM COMMANDS.

DEL	rm
Purpose	
These commands removes files.	
Usage	
DEL *FILE SWITCHES*	**rm *options file(s)***
Switches	**Options**
/P Verifies that the file is indeed to be deleted. (New in DOS 4.0.)	**–f** Removes files without verifying action with user.
	–i Removes files after verification from user. (New in System V Release 4.)
	–r Recursively moves through subdirectories. (Used when deleting directories.)

The Dangers of Erasing Files

As a DOS user, you've probably come to rely on some sort of utility to bail you out if you've accidentally erased some files. Utilities like *The Norton Utilities* and *PC Tools Deluxe* can "unerase" files that you've erased.

Although there's a version of *The Norton Utilities* for some versions of UNIX, by and large you can't rely on recovering any files you've erased on a UNIX system. UNIX uses a different of storing files on a

▼

disk than does DOS, and the tricks that a *PC Tools Deluxe* uses to unerase a file can't really be replicated easily on a UNIX filesystem.

There is, however, one potential out for you should you erase an essential file. Most UNIX system administrators—good ones, anyway—make frequent backups of the system. If you're lucky, there's an older version of your file sitting in an archive somewhere. While you probably will have lost some work, at least you don't need to start from scratch in recreating your work

The bottom line: If you deleting a file in UNIX, make damn sure you really do want to erase the file.

Working With Directories

You'll find that working with directories is similar to working with files. And that should come as no surprise—remember, UNIX directories are merely files that contain the names of other files and directories.

Creating Directories

DOS uses the **MKDIR** command to create directories. (The DOS command **MD** command also works, but this alternative is not frequently used, so you're forgiven if you're not familiar with it.) UNIX uses the **mkdir** command to create a file. Both commands are summarized in Table 4.6.

There's not much difference between the two commands. Both can be used to create a subdirectory within the current directory, or else they can be used to create a subdirectory within a directory other than the current directory, as in the following:

```
$ mkdir /users/kevin/reports
```

which would create a directory named **reports** in the directory **kevin**.

▼

When you create a directory, you must follow the rules that apply to naming files, which you learned in Chapter 3.

TABLE 4.6 COMMAND REFERENCES FOR THE MKDIR COMMANDS.

MKDIR	**mkdir**	
Purpose		
Creates a new directory.		
Usage		
MKDIR *DIRECTORY*	**mkdir** *directory*	
Switches	**Options**	
None.	**-m** *mode*	Specifies the *mode* of the new directory.

Copying Directories

One of the handier—and more unknown—DOS commands is **XCOPY**, which is essentially an extended version of the **COPY** command. **XCOPY** can be used to copy the contents of a directory to diskettes, or it can be used to copy directories, including all files and subdirectories found within.

For instance, the following command line will copy the contents of the directory **KEVIN**, including all subdirectories, to the directory **GEISHA**:

```
C:\WINDOWS> XCOPY \KEVIN\*.* \GEISHA /S
```

The contents of the **KEVIN** directory will remain intact. However, the files contained directly in **KEVIN** will appear as files contained within **GEISHA**. **KEVIN** does not become a subdirectory of **GEISHA**, although any subdirectories found within **KEVIN** will appear as subdirectories within **GEISHA**. (This is why **XCOPY** is not a widely used command. It can be very confusing at times.)

In UNIX, there are a few routes one can take for copying the contents of a directory. System V Release 4 users, for example, could use the **cp** command and the *–r* option to copy the contents of a directory, including subdirectories, into another directory:

```
$ cp -r /users/geisha /users/kevin
```

A quasiworkable alternative—especially for those who aren't using System V Release 4—involves the usage of the **tar** command. Originally intended as a tool for creating archives on a tape backup system (hence, the name—tape *archive*), **tar** can also be used to create backups of complete directories. Instead of creating an archive on a tape drive, the archive is essentially copied to another location in the filesystem.

However, there's a trick here (the first of many, actually): **tar** creates an archive by combining the files and compressing them into a single file. Before you can use the files in the new location, you must convert the archive back into the individual files and directories. Hence, copying a directory in this fashion is really two steps.

At this point in your UNIX education, you haven't been exposed to the notion of *pipes*. A pipe is merely a command line that commands two or more commands. Pipes will be explained in Chapter 5; for now, just be aware that the following command lines may look odd, but will work just fine.

Tar also is challenging because of its weird syntax—weird even by UNIX standards. Essentially, **tar** forces you to list the *destination* of the archive before the directories to be archived. This is an oddity in UNIXdom: Usually, the name of files to be acted upon comes immediately after the command and any options. To add to the quirkiness of the command, **tar** includes both function options—one of which must be a part of any list of options—and regular options, which follow function options. All in all, this leads to some pretty weird-looking command lines, as you'll see.

With all of this in mind, a command line that copies the contents of the directory **/users/kevin** into the directory **/users/geisha** using **tar** would look like this:

```
$ tar -cvf /users/geisha /users/kevin
```

To extract this archive, you would use the following command line:

```
$ tar -xvf /users/kevin
```

The full **tar** command is referenced in Table 4.7. As you can tell, **tar** is an extremely complex and confusing command, so use it with great caution.

TABLE 4.7 COMMAND REFERENCE FOR THE TAR COMMAND.

tar *options file(s)*

Purpose

The **tar command** archives files to **tar** files, often on backup tapes. (In UNIX, a tape isn't always a tape—in this instance, it may be a tape, hard disk, or diskette.) Specified files can either replace existing files or be appended to existing files. **Tar** is also used to extract archived files from tape.

The usage for the **tar** command differs slightly from the rest of the UNIX command set. Options have two parts: A function option (each command must contain of these), followed by other options. In addition, the hyphen (–) is not needed before options.

Function Options

c	Creates a new **tar** archive.
r	Appends *files* to the end of the archive.
t	Prints out a table of contents.
u	Updates archive by appending *files* if not on the tape or if they have been modified.
x	Extracts files from within the **tar** archive.

Options

bn	Sets blocking factor to *n* (default is 1; maximum is 64).
f dev	Writes archive to *dev*; default is **/dev/mt0** on many systems.
l	Returns error messages about links that cannot be read.
L	Follows symbolic links.
m	Updates file-modification times to the time of extraction.
o	Changes ownership of extracted files to the current user. This is very useful if the archive was made by another user.
v	Verbose mode: print out status information.
w	Wait for confirmation.

Removing Directories

The march of the similarities continues when you remove directories in both DOS and UNIX: DOS uses **RMDIR** (or, as an infrequent alternative, **RD**), while UNIX uses **rmdir**.

Both work pretty much the same, also. Neither command will remove a directory that contains either a file or directory. (This includes hidden files in both operating systems; you covered hidden commands in Chapter 3.) Neither will remove the current directory; your current directory must be other than the directory you want to remove.

To remove a directory in DOS, your command line would look like this:

```
C:\WINDOWS> RMDIR \KEVIN
```

To remove a directory in UNIX, your command line would look like this:

```
$ rmdir /kevin
```

The commands are compared in Table 4.8.

TABLE 4.8 REMOVING DIRECTORIES.

RMDIR	**rmdir**	
Purpose		
These commands will remove a directory, but only if the directory has no contents.		
Usage		
RMDIR *DIRECTORY*	**rmdir *directory***	
Switches	**Options**	
None.	**–p**	Removes the directory and any parent directory that is empty as a result of the action.
	–s	Ignores error messages.

Bright DOS users also know that the **DELTREE** command can be used to take out a directory and any subdirectories. It will quickly wipe out a specified directory and any subdirectories or files contained within, although it will make sure that you do indeed want to wipe out the information:

```
C:\> DELTREE \KEVIN
```

The **rm** command, which you've already seen applied to the removal of files, can also be used to remove a directory. (Remember, a directory is nothing more than a file that contains other filenames.)

If you're feeling confident and/or lucky, you can use **rm** in conjunction with a rather dangerous option: –r. Using this command line will remove the directory as well as any files and directories contained within. The command line:

```
$ rm -fr data
```

will remove the directory **data** as well as all its contents without giving you as much as a boo. (If you want to be asked before the system takes out a file or directory, drop the *f* option.) Again, this method isn't recommended unless you're really sure you want to remove the directory and its contents.

This Chapter in Review

▲ The similarities between UNIX and DOS continue, as this chapter reviews wildcards and a slew of commands that work directly with files and directories.

▲ For instance, both UNIX and DOS use the asterisk (*) and question-mark (?) wildcards to substitute for a character or set of characters.

▲ UNIX also goes a step further in wildcards by adding the set wildcard, which allows you to specify a range of characters.

▲ Other common DOS file commands have an almost-exact twin in the UNIX world, often to the point of sharing the same name.

▲   For example, both DOS and UNIX use the command **RMDIR** and **MKDIR** to remove and create directories, although they do differ on the case of the commands.

▲   To copy a file, DOS uses **COPY** while UNIX uses **cp**. Similarly, to remove a file, DOS uses **DEL**, while UNIX uses **rm**.

▲   The DOS command **XCOPY**, which copies a directory and all its contents, including subdirectories, has cousins in the UNIX world in **cp –r** (which copies a directory and all its contents) and **tar**, which creates an archive and can also be used for making copies of files and directories.

▲   Even some obscure DOS commands can be replicated in UNIX. For instance, the lesser-known **DELTREE** command has a counterpart in the **rm** command, provided you use the *–r* option with it.

An inability to develop an adequate multiuser system led to their decline.

▪ CHAPTER FIVE ▪
Peaceful Coexistence:
Multiuser Issues

One of the biggest distinguishing features of the UNIX operating system is its ability to support several users at one time. This support begins with the ability to keep track of many users at one time and extends through the ability to customize an individual environment and ends with the ability to run more than one command from a single user at one time. Topics covered in this chapter include:

▲ How UNIX supports multiple users

▲ Logging in a typical UNIX system installation

▲ Setting a new password

▲ Your home directory

▲ Learning about your shell

▲ Changing shells

▲ Changing your environment

▲ Working with shell variables

▲ Using redirection of standard input/output in your daily work

▲ Using pipes to combine commands

▲ Running more than one command at once

▲ Commands that rely on multitasking, including **at** and **nohup**

Peaceful Coexistence on a **UNIX** System

For the most part, DOS users are islands unto themselves. They aren't connected directly to other users, and they don't need to worry about the needs of other users.

This is not the case on the vast majority of UNIX systems. Indeed, the entire point of UNIX from the beginning was to support a number of users. As a result, there's a lot of rigmarole you must go through just to start a UNIX session. And the need to support multiple users adds a level of complexity to the UNIX operating system that simply isn't present in DOS. (On the flip side, the mechanisms that support multiple users running multiple applications has the potential to add a lot of power to your computing sessions. You win some, you lose some.)

Logging In a **UNIX** System

Before you can do any work with a UNIX system—even if you're the only user—you need to first tell the system that you're ready to work. Typically, the UNIX system is always running, and so your terminal is always active in some way. (Depending on your system setup, you may have to hit a key to get a display or turn on a power switch for the monitor itself. The procedures listed here are general in nature; your specific system setup may differ. As always, your friendly system administrator is the one to talk to about specifics on your system.)

You announce your presence to the system through a **login**. At this time, you'll enter your **username** and your **password**. (Gee, turning on a PC and waiting for DOS and perhaps *Windows* to boot was never this complicated, was it?) You'll see a screen looking like the one shown in Figure 5.1.

Depending on your system setup and UNIX vendor, your login screen may look different. (In fact, your login screen is *guaranteed* to look different than the one shown in Figure 5.1.) However, all login screens share two requirements in common: A username and a password.

```
ReallyBigCorp., Inc.
UNIX System V Release 4

login: kreichard
password: |
```

FIGURE 5.1 A typical login screen.

Typically, both your username and password will be initially assigned to you by your system administrator. Your username will often be an abbreviated version of your given name; for instance, the username *kreichard* shown in Figure 5.1 is short for *Kevin Reichard*. The closer to your real name, the better. While you may think it is cool to have a username of *attila_the_hun* (especially if you're a lawyer), a name like that is hard for other users to remember.

A password is a more serious matter, as you'll see in the following section.

Entering the information at the login screen is easy: You enter your username and press **Enter**. The cursor will move to the *password*: line, where you enter your password. The system will display your username as you type it in, but not your password. Why? Because of *security*. Throughout this book, the issue of security has been hammered home, and the issue of passwords on UNIX systems is a very delicate and important issue.

Reality Check: Logging In a System

If you should have trouble logging in a UNIX system, there are a few steps you can take to solve the problem:

▲　　If you make a mistake when typing in the username or password, you can either use the **BackSpace** (or **BkSp**) key to go back and reenter the correct letter. Or, you can take the lazy approach: Go ahead and enter the incorrect information, knowing full well that the system will tell you your login was incorrect. In this instance, the system will ask you to login again.

▲　　If the system tells you that your login was incorrect (or something to that effect; for reasons of security, UNIX systems tend to be somewhat vague when it comes to explanations of why logins fail), it will also give you a chance to reenter a username and password. If the second try also fails, check with your system administrator and make sure you're using the correct username and password.

▲　　If the username and password is seemingly accepted by the system and then nothing happens, be patient; UNIX systems can sometimes be balky during times of high workloads. If you've waited a few minutes and nothing happens, check with others around you to see if their systems are working before calling your system administrator to complain.

Passwords and Security Concerns

If someone has your password, they can get into your UNIX computer system. Every user represents a possible security breach, and there are many, *many* UNIX systems where security is a prime concern.

Getting the password of an existing user is the easiest way for a hacker to get into your company's UNIX system. There are a number of ways hackers can do this. One prime method is to merely look over the shoulder of a fellow worker and steal their password. (Not that you shouldn't trust your fellow workers, but the only person to trust when it comes to passwords is your system administrator.) This is why you should always be *very* careful with your password. Even though you'll be tempted to do so at first, don't write it down on a Post-It note and then stick it onto your monitor so you'll be able to see it when you're logging in the system. Don't write it down on a piece of paper and leave it next to your keyboard. Hide it so no one can find it if you should walk away from your desk.

Changing Your Password

You may want to change your password at some point to a string of characters that are more familiar to you. In addition, some systems force their users to change their passwords regularly in order to increase security. (This capability is actually built into the UNIX operating system; the system administrator can tell the system to force users to change passwords every so often.) In this instance, passwords are said to *age* and must be replaced every so often. In addition, you may want to change your password from the password originally assigned by the system administrator when your account was installed.

There's no such thing as total privacy on a UNIX system. Passwords are stored in a central location and in such a manner that the system administrator has the power to see an encrypted list of these passwords.

To change your password, use the **passwd** command, which is summarized in Table 5.1. The command is rather simple: After you login the system, you run the command and enter the new information when requested:

```
$ passwd
UX: passwd: changing password for kevin
Old password:
New password:
```

```
Re-enter new password:
$
```

As when entering your password while logging in the system, the **passwd** doesn't display your password as you enter it.

TABLE 5.1 COMMAND REFERENCE FOR THE PASSWD COMMAND.

passwd *options*

passwd *options user* (**privileged users**)

Purpose

The **passwd** command sets or changes your password.

Options

–s Displays current password information:

user	User name.
status	Password status: **NP** (no password), **PS** (password), or **LK** (locked).
mm/dd/yy	Date when last changed.
min	Minimum number of days before password must be changed.
max	Maximum number of days before password must be changed.
notice	Number of days before you are given notice that your password must be changed.

 The –s option is available only in the newest versions of UNIX.

SCO UNIX users have one additional option to the **passwd** command: You can have the system randomly generate a password for you if you prefer. In addition, the system will also ask you if you want a pronounceable password.

Many users confuse the **pwd** command with the **passwd** command. As you'll recall from Chapter 3, the **pwd** command returns the name of the current working directory.

Choosing a New Password

When you run the **passwd** command to change your password, there are a few rules you must follow when choosing a new password:

▲　　The new password must be more than two characters, and usually not more than eight characters.

▲　　Make sure your password is longer than six characters. Shorter passwords are easier to decipher by either random chance or determined individuals.

▲　　Your password must contain two alphabetic characters and one numeral or special character (**!**, **@**, **#**, etc.), generally speaking. Some older UNIX systems, however, don't allow the use of nonalphabetic characters, and some PC-based UNIX systems, such as UnixWare, don't require a numeral. If you're trying to enter a new password and the system won't accept it, check with your system administrator.

▲　　*Never* use a password based solely on personal information. A popular tool for system hackers is to try personal names as passwords, on the theory that someone would have entered their lover's name as a password. In addition, don't use your middle name, your spouse's name, your child's name, or your job title as a password.

▲　　Don't use words that are easily guessed, such as **sun**, **boss**, **password**, or anything else obvious.

▲ On the other hand, don't make your password too complicated. This is a string that you'll need to remember, after
all—if you make it too complex, you'll probably just write it
on a sheet of paper and leaving it next to your terminal,
which means that anyone walking by your terminal can
probably see your password. (Indeed, this author has seen
instances where users have written their passwords on Post-
It notes and then attached the Post-It note to the terminal
screen.) The best advice is to use two easily remembered
words in combination—making sure that the two portions
of the password aren't related. For instance, you may think
Rush Limbaugh is full of hot air, so you choose *rush* and *hot*
as elements for your password. This isn't a valid password—
remember, you need at least one numeral—but a password
of *rushhot1* certainly would be. (*Rushhotair1* would be an
even better password.)

▲ There's a neat trick used by many UNIX users over the years
that turns passwords into gibberish, but still keeps them easy
to remember. Choose a word or phrase that means something to you, like *passion*. Now look at your keyboard. For
your real password, use the keys to the upper-left of the keys
spelling out *passion*. In this case, the first letter of *passion*, *p*,
becomes *0*, and *passion* becomes *0qww89h*, your real password. No one is going to ever hack *0qww89h* as a password.

The UNIX Home Directory

When you login a UNIX system, you're placed at a specific location in
the directory structure. This is called your **home directory**, and it contains most of the files that define your UNIX usage. Users, as well as
files, must exist within a directory. In theory, this directory contains
the files you need to complete your work. This might include letters
and memos, as well as the files that define your personal usage.

In your home directory is a file called **.profile**. This file contains
information about your UNIX usage. A sample **.profile** file—the
default **.profile** file from UnixWare, by the way—is as follows.

```
MAIL=/var/mail/${LOGNAME:?}
. $HOME/.olsetup        #!@ Do not edit this line !@
```

This **.profile** file doesn't do much, to be honest. (This has to do with the structures used by UnixWare—a version of UNIX designed for personal computers—and little to do with the actual role of the **.profile** file. Your **.profile** files will probably be longer and more involved.)

 You have the ability to edit these **.login** and **.profile** files to customize your environment. However, you don't want to be messing with these files at the beginning of your great UNIX journey. Editing these files is a matter for a more experienced view of the UNIX word.

At this point, your biggest concern with your home directory is as a repository for your work files. Indeed, you have the ability to create and delete directories and files within your home directory, and the idea is to organize these files in an orderly fashion. Take a look at Figure 5.2, which shows a portion of a typical UNIX filesystem.

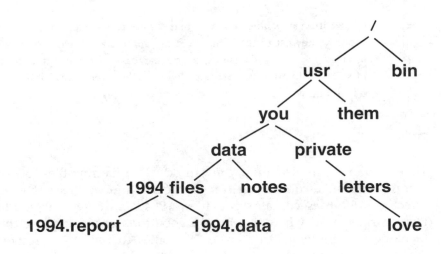

FIGURE 5.2 A portion of a typical UNIX filesystem.

In this case, the directory **you** represents your home directory. Within the directory named **you**, there are two subdirectories, **data** and **private**. Within the directory **data**, there are two subdirectories, **1994files** and **notes**, while the subdirectory **letters** is within the **private** directory. The intent here, obviously, is to separate personal correspondence from the corporate correspondence. The philosophy can be extended to other categories of files; for instance, electronic-mail messages from fellow employees can be filed in a directory named **email**, while memos from your boss can be filed in a directory named **memos**.

Don't worry about creating too many subdirectories: The UNIX system places few limits on the number of subdirectories you can produce. And paying attention to how your files are organized is one the real tricks of efficient UNIX usage: You'll be surprised at the number of files you end up creating over a few months, and you'll also be surprised to see how quickly you forget about most of them. This is also why it's important to be careful about how you name files. There's no required link between the contents of the file and the filename. For instance, a file containing a list of apple trees could be called **oranges**. Or a file containing a list of customers could be called **suckers**.

The unwritten rule, however, says that the contents of a file should correspond somewhat to the filename. Programmers work with some specific rules containing filenames, as do database-management experts. And so should you, if you want to keep track of the many UNIX files you'll end up generating in the course of your daily work.

There are a few simple things you can do when naming files to help you track them, also. Refer again to Figure 5.2, and you'll see that the directory **1994files** contains two files, **1994.report** and **1994.data**. Placing a date somewhere in a file is a good tool for making sure that filenames are individualistic—when it comes to routine correspondence, you can place the date somewhere in the filename, such as **memo.612** or **letters.1212**.

Getting Back To the Home Directory

When you first login a UNIX system, your current directory and your home directory are one and the same. However, should you change your current directory, you'll leave your home directory behind.

If you ever want to move back to your home directory—in essence, making your home directory your current directory—you can do so with the **cd** command, used by itself on a command line. When you fail to specify a new destination directory with **cd**, you'll automatically be placed in your home directory.

The exact commands in the form of an example are shown in Figure 5.3.

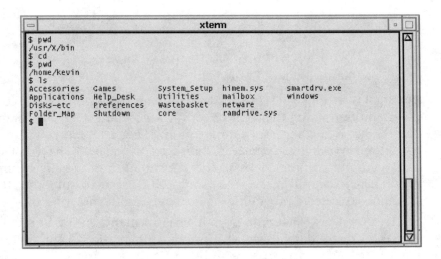

```
                              xterm
$ pwd
/usr/X/bin
$ cd
$ pwd
/home/kevin
$ ls
Accessories   Games        System_Setup  himem.sys    smartdrv.exe
Applications  Help_Desk    Utilities     mailbox      windows
Disks-etc     Preferences  Wastebasket   netware
Folder_Map    Shutdown     core          ramdrive.sys
$
```

FIGURE 5.3 Moving to the home directory.

This is one instance where DOS and UNIX differ, despite featuring the same command. If you were to use the DOS **CD** command on a single command line, you'd see something like the following:

```
C:\WINDOWS> CD
C:\WINDOWS
```

As you can see, the DOS **CD** command returns the name of the current directory. It will not move you anywhere else on the filesystem, as the UNIX **cd** command does.

Learning About Your Shell

When you login a UNIX system, one of the first things the system sets up for you is the proper **shell**. A shell is a program specially designed to act as a buffer between you and the UNIX system. When you enter commands into the UNIX system, you're actually giving a command to a shell, which in turn tells the UNIX system exactly what to do.

You can choose which shell you use; there's no requirement that every user on the system use the same shell. There are many different shells available, including (but not limited to):

- ▲ C shell (**csh**)
- ▲ Korn shell (**ksh**)
- ▲ Bourne shell (**sh**)
- ▲ Windowing Korn shell (**wksh**)
- ▲ Public-domain Korn shell (**pdksh**)

The shell is responsible for taking the commands you enter in the computer and translating them into a form the computer can understand. The shell also encompasses a programming language that you can use to customize your environment. (Don't worry—you won't have to tackle programming in the course of this book.) But there are a few things you can do that will make your daily UNIX usage go smoother that might be considered programming on a very rudimentary level.

The shell also determines your **environment**: Information that determines your daily usage and system configuration. Your environment is specific to your usage. No other UNIX user on the system will have your same exact environment.

Shell Games

Almost every UNIX system comes with a variety of shells. While you'll probably stick with the shell already set up for your use—at least in the initial stages of your UNIX usage—it's good to know what alternatives are out there.

UNIX is rather unique in that it separates the shell from the under-lying operating system. DOS includes a file called **COMMAND.COM** that is the functional equivalent of the UNIX shell. You're probably already familiar with **COMMAND.COM** (indeed, its presence is pretty hard to miss) in some fashion, especially if you've ever installed DOS. However, DOS users are stuck with the **COMMAND.COM** file that ships with their version of DOS.

By contrast, UNIX users can choose their own shells, even on the fly if they so desire. The most popular shell is the oldest major shell: The Bourne shell, named after its creator, Stephen Bourne. The Bourne shell (with a filename of **sh**) is pretty much the same as when Bourne introduced it in 1979.

The first real competitor to the Bourne shell came from Bill Joy (a founder of Sun Microsystems, Inc.) while at the University of California at Berkeley. His alternative, the C shell (with a filename of **csh**), is also very popular these days. In many ways, the C shell resem-bles the popular C programming language that is the foundation of the UNIX operating system. It also contains a few neat features, like job history and aliases, that were not found in the Bourne shell. Though this chapter focuses on shell usage in general, C shell com-mands and procedures will be outlined when they differ from Korn or Bourne shell commands and procedures.

The last of the Big Three Shells is the Korn shell (with a filename of **ksh**), written by David Korn of Bell Laboratories. The Korn shell was designed as a direct extension to the Bourne shell, which means that scripts and programs written for the Bourne shell can be used under the Korn shell without modifications. (By contrast, the C shell uses differ-ent built-in commands than do the Bourne and Korn shells.) In addi-tion, the Korn shell also implemented many popular features, such as job history and aliases, that had been introduced in the Bourne shell.

Things like *job history* and *aliases* will be more important when you become a more experienced user. For the time being, they are not important to your daily computing chores.

Shells on Your System

As mentioned earlier, you'll probably want to stick with the shell already set up for your use. Although you may benefit from some of the advanced features of the Korn and C shells further in your UNIX usage, your initial shell needs will be so basic that the shell you use won't really matter. If you're curious about which shell is installed in your system, use the following command line:

```
$ echo $SHELL
```

The response will be **sh**, **csh**, **ksh**, or some other name ending in *sh*. If you want to use a different shell, you must first see what shells are available in your system. Generally, shell programs can be found in the **/usr/bin** or **/bin** directories, and their filenames end with *sh*.

Some UNIX vendors don't ship the Bourne shell as such; instead, they ship the Korn shell under the filename **sh**.

To see what shells are available on your system, you can try the following command:

```
$ ls /usr/bin/*sh
/usr/bin/csh   /usr/bin/ksh   /usr/bin/sh
```

The response to the above command line indicates that there are three shells (**csh**, **ksh**, and **sh**) installed on the system. However, you may receive a different response, more like the following:

```
$ ls /usr/bin/*sh
UX: *sh: No such file or directory exists
```

This command line makes use of a wildcard, which you already know about through your DOS usage. In this instance, the actual shell files may be stored elsewhere on the UNIX filesystem. Check with your system administrator to see where shell files are stored and if you can have access to them.

At any point in your UNIX usage, you can start a new shell. For instance, if you're currently using the C shell and want to switch to the Korn shell, you can enter the following command line:

```
% ksh
$
```

As noted in Chapter 2, the system uses a special character, named a prompt, to indicate that the system is ready for your input. If you're using the Korn or Bourne shells, your prompt looks like this:

```
$
```

If you're using the C shell, your prompt looks like this:

```
%
```

or

```
spike%
```

where *spike* is the name of the computer. If you're using the Windowing Korn shell, your prompt will look like this:

```
[WKSH]
```

The shell allows you to change your prompt, as the shell controls the character used to designate the prompt. You may want to change the prompt to look more like the DOS prompt (>). In this case (assuming you're a Korn or Bourne shell user), you'd enter the following command in your system:

```
$ PS1="> "
```

This command changes the string **$** to the string **>**, with a space after the > sign. (The space ensures that your commands don't abut the prompt—a move to cut down on potential confusion more than anything else.) The quotation marks are used by the system to frame characters to be printed, making sure that the shell knows that the characters within the quotation marks aren't part of the actual command. (In UNIX command lines, characters to be displayed on the screen are bracketed by quotation marks.) The resulting prompt would look like this:

```
>
```

The change to the prompt applies only to your account and won't affect other users. You can use this command line at any point in your daily UNIX usage. However, it applies only to your current computing session; after you log off the system, the prompt will revert to the default.

If you're using the C shell, the following command changes a prompt:

```
% set prompt = "> "
```

In short, the shell controls all interaction between you and the system—but it also allows you to make a lot of changes in the exact interaction. A good example is changing the **Delete** key.

Changing the Delete Key

One of the more useful changes you can make via the shell makes sure that the **Delete** key actually deletes text. Older UNIX systems were rather cavalier regarding the needs of users. Instead of having a designated **Delete** key—no matter what the labels on the keyboard said—these systems would feature awkward key combinations like **Ctrl-H** or **#** (**Shift-3**). Using the **#** character to erase a character gets old quickly; the character is still displayed on your terminal, and if you make a lot of typos, you'll have to wade through a lot of **#** characters to figure out exactly what you typed.

If you can't figure out what key is used to delete a character or just you want to make sure that they key labeled **Delete** actually deletes characters, you can actually change the key used to delete characters. This is an old tradition within the UNIX world and still is common today.

To change the delete-character key, use the **stty erase** command line. The usage is simple: Type *stty*, then a *space*, then *erase*, then a space, then you press the key that you want to delete characters (for our purposes, we'll use the obvious choice of the **Del** key, although you could use any key on your keyboard if you want), and then press the **Enter** key. The resulting command line would look like this:

▼

```
$ stty erase [Del]
```

where *[Del]* is the key assigned to the task of deleting characters.

Your Files

Since everything concerning UNIX is contained in a file, it also follows logically that information about *you* is stored within a file. UNIX doesn't know you from Mark Twain when you sit down and login at a terminal. When you enter your username, you're telling the UNIX system who you are, verifying that information with a password. The system then takes that information to look up information about you in several files.

As you saw in the previous section, a file named **.profile** does a few things when you login the system. In addition, a file named **.login** also sets some system information after you login the system.

You have the ability to edit these **.login** and **.profile** files to customize your environment. However, you don't want to be messing with these files at the beginning of your great UNIX journey. Editing these files is a matter for a more experienced view of the UNIX word.

Until you get more comfortable with your UNIX system, it's best not to be messing with your configuration files. To increase your comfort level, however, you can see the type of things you can change in your system configuration without making these changes permanent. To do this, you can make some changes to your system configuration through the use of variables.

Variables

Those with more than a hazy recollection of their high-school days should recognize a reference to *variables*. In the following line:

125

▼

```
z=x+y
```

z, *x*, and *y* are all variables. The value of all three can change, depending on input from within the equation or from the reader.

UNIX uses variables the same way: Users can define information with both a name and a value that may change under various circumstances. The shell, in particular, uses variables often. For instance: Earlier in this chapter, an example **.profile** file contains the following line:

```
MAIL=/var/mail/${LOGNAME:?}
```

This line sets up the MAIL variable. When the shell or another UNIX application looks for the location to store MAIL, it knows through this variable where to send the information. Variables control the type of terminal you're using, what your system prompt is (as you'll recall, you changed the system prompt earlier in this chapter), and applications that will run right after you login the system.

All of your current variables are set by the system and your system administrator. There may be times when you'll want to change a variable. To do so, you'd use the following command-line syntax:

```
$ VARIABLENAME=VARIABLEVALUE
```

where *VARIABLENAME* is the name of the variable you want to change, and *VARIABLEVALUE* is the new value.

This is technical

One of the most common changes a new user will make has to do with the **terminal** type. This situation occurs when you're using a terminal different than what the system thinks you're using, resulting in bad communications and errors between your terminal and the system. (You'll see the errors on the screen—it will look like gibberish—and sometimes what you type in the keyboard won't appear accurately on the screen.) While you don't need to know exactly why this variable needs resetting, you should know that you have the power to set it.

To change the terminal variable to the nearly universal VT100 terminal type, using the following command line:

```
$ TERM=vt100
```

To see a listing of your current variables, use the **set** command:

```
$ set
CODEPAGE=pc437
CONSEM=no
COUNTRY=1
DESKTOPDIR=/home/kevin
DISPLAY=spike:0.0
DT=yes
HOME=/home/kevin
HZ=100
KEYB=us
LANG=C
LC_CTYPE=C
LC_MESSAGES=C
LC_NUMERIC=C
LC_TIME=C
LD_LIBRARY_PATH=:/usr/X/lib
LOGNAME=kevin
MAIL=/var/mail/kevin
MAILCHECK=600
OPTIND=1
PATH=/usr/bin:/usr/dbin:/usr/ldbin:/usr/X/bin
PS1=$
PS2=>
SHELL=/usr/bin/sh
TERM=xterm
TERMCAP=/etc/termcap
TFADMIN=
TIMEOUT=0
TZ=:US/Central
WINDOWID=29360164
XDM_LOGIN=yes
XGUI=MOTIF
XWINHOME=/usr/X
```

This is a rather extensive set of variables. Most of them won't mean a thing to you. However, there are a few that are worth noting.

The **set** command is explained in Table 5.2.

TABLE 5.2 COMMAND REFERENCE FOR THE SET COMMAND.

> **set *options***
>
> **Purpose**
>
> The **set** command lists the current variables when it is used with no options. While there are several options available, most are of use to shell programmers or advanced users.
>
> **Options**
>
> **–a**   Exports changes to variables (not available on all systems).

Some C shell users can use the same command. However, the output will look different:

```
spike% set
argv    ()
cwd     /home/kevin
home    /home/kevin
path    (/usr/bin /usr/dbin /usr/ldbin /usr/X/bin)
prompt  spike%
shell   /bin/csh
status  0
term    xterm
```

If the **set** command doesn't work on your system, try using **setenv** or **env** (which is explained in Table 5.3):

```
% env
CODEPAGE=pc437
CONSEM=no
COUNTRY=1
DESKTOPDIR=/home/kevin
DISPLAY=spike:0.0
DT=yes
HOME=/home/kevin
HZ=100
```

```
KEYB=us
LANG=C
LC_CTYPE=C
LC_MESSAGES=C
LC_NUMERIC=C
LC_TIME=C
LD_LIBRARY_PATH=:/usr/X/lib
LOGNAME=kevin
MAIL=/var/mail/kevin
PATH=/usr/bin:/usr/dbin:/usr/ldbin:/usr/X/bin
SHELL=/usr/bin/sh
TERM=xterm
TERMCAP=/etc/termcap
TFADMIN=
TIMEOUT=0
TZ=:US/Central
WINDOWID=29360164
XDM_LOGIN=yes
XGUI=MOTIF
XWINHOME=/usr/X
PWD=/home/kevin
```

There are a few lines in the previous examples that at first glance seem to be in error, such as:

```
PATH=/usr/bin:/usr/dbin:/usr/ldbin:/usr/X/bin
```

This is not an error. Rather, the variable encompasses more than one item. In this case, the PATH variable tells the shell where to look for filenames. Since there is more than one directory containing commands, the system is set up to look in more than one directory. In this example, colons (:) are used to distinguish between multiple options.

TABLE 5.3 COMMAND REFERENCE FOR THE ENV COMMAND.

env *option [variable=value] command*

Purpose

The **env** command displays the current user environment variables with their values, or makes changes to environment variables for users of the C shell.

Option

– Ignores the current set of environment variables.

All in all, there's a lot of information you'll need to wade through when using the **set/setenv/env** commands. Most of it will be utterly meaningless to you. (In the previous examples, most of the information had to do with the specific needs of UnixWare.) However, there are a few shell variables that you should know about, and they are listed in Tables 5.4 and 5.5.

TABLE 5.4 SHELL VARIABLES FOR THE BOURNE AND KORN SHELLS.

Variable	Meaning
CDPATH	Directories that are automatically searched when you use the **cd** command.
HOME	The full name of your home directory.
LOGNAME	Your login name.
MAIL	The directory where your electronic-mail messages are stored.
PATH	Directories that are automatically searched by the shell when you issue a command to the system.
SHELL	The full filename of your current shell.
TERM	Your terminal type.
TZ	Your current time zone.
USER	Your login name (used instead of LOGNAME on some systems).

TABLE 5.5   SHELL VARIABLES FOR THE C SHELL.

Variable	Meaning
cdpath	Directories that are automatically searched when you use the **cd** command.
HOME	The full name of your home directory.
mail	The directory where your electronic-mail messages are stored.
PATH	Directories that are automatically searched by the shell when you issue a command to the system.
prompt	Sets the characters used in the prompt.
TERM	Your terminal type.
USER	Your login name (used instead of LOGNAME on some systems).

When working with variables, there are a few things to remember:

▲   Remember at all times: *case counts*. TERM, Term, and term would be three different variables. While you can use your own variables (a subject you'll cover in the next section), the system's reserved variables all are in uppercase letters.

▲   When using a variable on the command line, you must preface it with a dollar sign (**$**), as you did earlier in this chapter when checking for the shell currently in use:

```
$ echo $SHELL
/usr/bin/ksh
```

The dollar sign (**$**) tells the shell that you're specifying the value of a variable on the command line, rather than a command or an option to a command.

▲   The above use of the **echo** command can be used to check for the value of *any* variable. Instead of wading through the information returned by the **set** command when looking for a specific variable, you can simply use **echo**, as in the following:

```
$ echo $TERM
xterm
```

Setting Your Own Variables

You aren't limited to the variables initially supported by the system. While the notion of setting up your own variables seems to be too complicated a notion, there are several situations where you will find that your own variables are very convenient.

For instance: You're working on an involved project and want to store all of the files in the same directory, buried deep within the directory tree: **/users/kevin/data/reports/research/1994**. This is a mighty long directory name to type every time you want to store or call a file. In this case, you can assign a variable to this long directory name. To do so, you'd use the following command line:

```
$ DATA="/users/kevin/data/reports/research/1994"
```

Here, the use of the DATA variable is totally arbitrary: You could use variable names of REPORTS or FILES, as long as the name you choose isn't already in use by the system. (To find out which names are in use, you can use the **set** command, a process outlined earlier in this chapter.)

In the above command line, you'll notice that the name of the directory was in quotation marks. Any string you save as a variable must be placed in quotation marks.

Exporting Variables

When you create a variable as you did above, you're making sure it can be used by the shell. Similarly, when you change a system variable, you're making the change to the shell. In both cases, you're not necessarily making the change apply to any applications you're using.

To make sure that your changes can be used throughout your UNIX computing experience, use the export command:

```
$ export DATA
```

You can export multiple variables on the same command line:

```
$ export DATA TERM PATH
```

When you assign your own variable, you can also export it on the same command line:

```
$ DATA="/users/kevin/reports/research/1994"; export data
```

If you're exporting *every* variable you assign or change, you can use an option to the set command to make these assignments automatic:

```
$ set -a
```

Removing Your Variables

If you are finished with variables, you can remove them from the system with the **unset** command:

```
$ unset DATA
```

This would remove variables defined by DATA. The **unset** command is summarized in Table 5.6.

TABLE 5.6 COMMAND REFERENCE FOR THE UNSET COMMAND.

unset *variable*

Purpose
The **unset** command literally unsets variables set by the user or the system.

Options
None.

Standard Input/Output

When you use commands like **set** and **unset**, the results of the command are automatically displayed to your monitor. Generally speaking, UNIX assumes that commands are entered from the keyboard (known as **standard input**), with the results displayed to the monitor (known as **standard output**). Together, standard input and standard output are commonly referred to as I/O. This reliance on jargon is a typically obtuse—typical for UNIX, at least—way of saying that things you type with the keyboard will appear on the screen.

Technically speaking, standard input/output has little to do with multi-user issues and UNIX. However, it is a function of the shell, so that's why it's included in this chapter.

DOS assumes the same thing, so you aren't dealing with anything that should be too unfamiliar. Indeed, if you're an advanced DOS user, you'll recognize many of the things explained in the remainder of this chapter. DOS supports things like redirection and pipes.

However, most DOS users are not advanced users. Most users have no need to wade in the depths of advanced DOS usage. Because most DOS users are application driven—in essence, using the operating system almost exclusively to run applications (including *Windows*, by the way), rather than using the operating system to perform some basic capabilities—things like standard I/O are lost on the typical DOS user.

UNIX, though, puts a great deal of stress on standard input/output and its usefulness to the average UNIX user. Indeed, a great amount of your work can eventually be automated or at least made easier through some smart use of the tools listed in the remainder of this chapter. So don't worry about being a DOS user and not being familiar with standard input/output. Just put the jargon behind and focus on the relatively simple concepts underlying standard input/output.

There are times when you'll want a command to receive input from another source (such as a file), and there are times when you'll want a command to send output to a place other than the monitor, such as a printer or a file. In these cases, you'll want to **redirect** the input or output. This redirection is performed as part of the command line and is quite simple to accomplish.

In fact, you'll find the ability to redirect input and output to be one of the handiest functions of the UNIX operating system. Unfortunately, this ability is generally ignored by beginning users, who tend to be put off by all the jargon associated with a very basic functionality—who would think that something appearing in the documentation as *standard input/output redirection* or *redirection I/O* could be so simple?

UNIX (as well as DOS, for that matter) uses the > and < characters to accomplish this simple redirection. For instance, you may want to save the results of the **ls** command to a file instead of the screen. This is probably the most common usage of redirection, since the information generated by many UNIX commands tend to run on the largish side, to say the least. Trying to pick a piece of information from rapidly scrolling text can be difficult at times, and it's much easier to save the information to a file and search through it with a text editor.

To send the results of the **ls** command to a file named *myfile* instead of the screen, you'd use the following command line:

```
$ ls > myfile
```

That's all there is to it. This will work with any command that sends its output to the screen. Once you have the results in a file, you can use any number of UNIX tools to view that information at a more leisurely pace—Chapter 6 covers many such tools.

There are other redirection tools, as explained in Table 5.7.

TABLE 5.7 SHELL REDIRECTION COMMANDS.

Symbol	Usage	Result
>	*command>filename*	The output of the command *command* is send to *filename*.
<	*command<filename*	The input from *filename* is used by *command*.
>>	*command>>filename*	The output from *command* is appended to *filename*.
|	*command1|command2*	First *command1* is run, and then the output is sent to *command2*.

Using some common UNIX commands, you'll better see redirection in action in Table 5.8.

TABLE 5.8 REDIRECTION IN ACTION.

Command	Result
ls > *filename*	The contents of the current directory, as listed with the **ls** command, are sent to *filename* rather than displayed on the screen. If *filename* doesn't exist, the shell will create it. If *filename* does exist, the results of the **ls** command will overwrite the existing data. In this instance, information from the **ls** command is used as input for the file *filename*.
cat <*filename*	The **cat** command displays the contents of the file *filename* on the screen. In this instance, *filename* is used as input for the **cat** command.
ls >>*filename*	The contents of the current directory, as listed with the **ls** command, are appended to the end of the file *filename*. In this instance, information from the **ls** command is used as input for the file *filename*.
ls | **lp**	The contents of the current directory, as listed with the **ls** command, are sent to the UNIX command **lp**, which prints the information. (The **lp** command will be covered later in this chapter.)

Reality Check: Redirection

UNIX does not like beginning or casual users. This is evident by the harm that can be caused by the seemingly innocent act of redirection.

What makes UNIX so unfeeling? Because it will wipe out files at the drop of a hat. For instance, if you use the following command:

```
$ ls > myfile
```

and there already existed a file named *myfile* in the directory, UNIX would have no qualms about wiping out the old *myfile* and replacing it with the new *myfile*. In UNIX jargon, the old file was *clobbered* (for once, the jargon is illuminating).

Pipes

Another feature in UNIX that is present in DOS, though underused, is the ability to combine commands in a way where the output of one command is the input of a second command. The idea of **pipes** takes redirection to a new level of functionality, but also a new level of complexity. While there are certainly times when pipes are convenient, don't worry if you're so intimidated by them that you never use them.

Put simply: A pipe acts as a conduit between two commands. With a pipe, you specify that the results of one command should be used as the input of a second command. In a sense, the pipe is a temporary file that hold data after it's been acted upon by one command and before it is used by a second command.

Setting up a **pipeline** is a simple matter:

```
$ command1 | command2
```

In this example, the output from *command1* is used as input for *command2*. The character in the middle is a vertical bar. (Aha! *This* is why that funny-looking character exists on keyboards!) While this example is limited to only two commands, there's no limit as to how many commands you can set up in a pipeline.

Most often, pipes—as well as redirection, for that matter—are used when printing documents with the **lp** command. The **lp** command is the UNIX command for printing. While there's a lot to learn about the **lp** command (which you'll do when you get to Chapter 8), in this instance, all you need to know is that the **lp** command is used for printing.

Let's say that you want to print the contents of a directory after generating them with the **ls** command. There are two ways to do it. You could generate the listing and then redirect the output to a file, and then you can print the file. There's nothing particularly wrong with this method, although it uses two steps to perform what should be a simple task. (It also has you creating a file, which means you must be certain to delete the file at some point.) Or you can directly print the results of the **ls** command, using a pipe, as in the following command line:

```
$ ls | lp
```

There's no limit as to how many commands you can connect with pipes.

Multitasking: Doing More Than One Thing At Once

One of the prime reasons UNIX has become such a popular operating system is its ability to do more than one thing at once.

As a DOS user, this is a totally new capability. DOS is a **single-tasking environment**, which means that the operating system does one thing at one time. *Windows* does allow you to be doing more than one thing at once, but does so through a series of tricks that makes it look as though multiple tasks are being carried out; in essence, *Windows* switches very quickly between tasks.

You've probably been frustrated by this limitation at some point in your DOS usage. You may have wanted to work while a large file was printing, only to find out that the system was tied up with the task of printing the document. You may have wanted to transfer a file from an online service, only to find that the system was tied up with the download.

With UNIX, you can be devoting your attention to one task—in the parlance, running the command in the **foreground**—while the system follows through with another command silently—in the parlance, running the other command in the **background**. Put together, this capability is called **multitasking**, and it's exactly what the name says: Running more than one task at once.

This is technical

Computer geeks love to argue about exactly what constitutes multitasking (as if anyone really cares about the difference between preemptive multitasking and timeslicing). Don't be sucked into arguments about multitasking. Just rest assured that UNIX features the most superior, purest form of multitasking.

From your viewpoint, multitasking, which is managed by the shell, is quite simple. When you enter a command in the system and tell the shell that you want to run the command in the background, the shell throws up another prompt, telling you that it's ready for another command while the background command chugs forth. In fact, depending on your system, the command can keep running even after you log off the system.

Running Commands in the Background

Running a command in the background is a simple matter: Add an ampersand (&) to the end of the command line. The shell then assigns a *process ID (PID)*, to the command and throws up a prompt, indicating that it's open for further commands:

```
$ sort file1 file2 > file.sort &
[1] 2445
$
```

In this case, you're sorting two files in the background. Sorting files—especially large files—can take quite a bit of time, so it's a good idea to run the **sort** command in the background.

Don't worry about the exact process ID. There's really no reason why you'll need to remember the number; if there is an occasion to reference the process ID, there are UNIX tools (which you'll cover below) that can retrieve the ID.

The shell will inform you when the background command is completed.

Listing Processes

There's no effective limit to how many commands you run in the background. There are also cases when you're running commands in the background when you don't realize it: For instance, if you're running the X Window System and a graphical interface, you're already running commands in the background automatically.

Still, there may be occasion when you want to check on the background command. You may have begun a large task and decide to cancel it, after deciding that the resulting task isn't worth the fuss. In this instance, you'll use the **ps** command to find the PID:

```
$ ps
     PID TTY        TIME COMD
     681 pts001    0:03 ps
     679 pts001    1:21 sh
$
```

There are four parts to this listing:

▲ The process ID (PID), which is the unique number assigned to the background command by the UNIX system

▲ The terminal (TTY) that originated the command

▲ The amount of time (TIME) the process has been running

▲ The command name (COMD)

You'll notice that the **ps** command also listed itself. In addition, the command will also list the shell as a current process. These listings will be present every time you run the **ps** command.

The output from the **ps** command on a larger UNIX system can be voluminous. You may want to send the results of this command to a file, using the wonderful redirection commands you've already covered in this book.

After you've run the **ps** command, you can use the information to kill the process. The UNIX command to do so, eerily enough, is **kill**. Using the results of the previous **ps** command as a reference, you can kill the **sort** command with the following command line:

```
$ kill 21087
```

The Command Reference for the **ps** command is listed in Table 5.9.

TABLE 5.9 COMMAND REFERENCE FOR THE PS COMMAND.

ps *options*

Purpose

The **ps** command lists the status of all current processes.

In BSD UNIX, the options are slightly different; for instance, use **ps –aux** instead of **ps –ef**. In these cases, check your system documentation.

Options

–a Displays all processes.

–d Displays all processes, except group leaders.

–e Displays information on every process.

–f Displays full information about processes, including **UID**, **PID**, **PPID**, **C**, **STIME**, **TTY**, **TIME**, and **COMMAND**.

–l Displays a long listing, which includes such information as priorities set with the **nice** command—and much, much more. (Don't use this option unless you are ready for a *very long* listing.)

Commands That Use Multitasking

With multitasking, you can set up commands to run in the background and essentially forget about them until they are through running. A few UNIX commands take advantage of this capability.

The Nice Command

Every UNIX should be a nice user. In this context, however, *nice* refers to a specific situation. When you use the **nice** command, you're telling the system to run the command at the system's leisure, not devoting a ton of system resources to the command. This command is quite useful when you're anticipating a long lunch and you want to sort that huge file so it's ready when you return.

A typical **nice** command line would look something like this:

```
$ nice option command argument(s)
```

where *command* is the name of the command you want to run nicely, *option* refers to the only option available with this command (don't worry—for the most part, you won't need to use this option), and argument(s) refers to the *argument(s)* you want the command to use as input. In short: You'd use your normal command line in conjunction with the **nice** command—the only difference is that you stick **nice** at the beginning of the command line.

The Command Reference for the **nice** command is listed in Table 5.10.

TABLE 5.10 THE COMMAND REFERENCE FOR THE NICE COMMAND.

nice *option command argument(s)*

Purpose

The **nice** command runs a command nicely, by giving it a very low priority.

Option

–n   Allows you to set a priority level for the command. The default is 10.

The At Command

The **at** command pretty much does exactly what the name implies: It runs a command line *at* a specified time.

In this instance, the UNIX command is keeping track of the **at** command as a current process, and when the specified time arrives, the **at** command then runs the command line.

There really aren't many circumstances where you'll need to use the **at** command. It's a handy thing to save computational-heavy commands for the middle of the night, when there's no one else using the system and no one to irritate when you're tying up the laser printer with a 2,000-page document. However, system administrators will find the command to be of greater use.

The **at** command is not available to every user on every system. In many cases, usage of this command is limited to system administrators. In these situations, you'll get the following error message when you try and use the **at** command:

```
at: you are not authorized to run at. Sorry.
```

To use the **at** command, you'll use it on its own command line in conjunction with the time you want a command line to run. For instance, the following command line would run a command at 11 p.m.:

```
$ at 11pm
```

After you press the **Return** or **Enter** key, the cursor will appear on the following line *without* a prompt. It's at this point that you'll enter the command line you want to run at 11 p.m. When you're through with the command line, press **Ctrl-D** to tell the **at** command that you're through entering the command line, *not* the **Enter** key.

You can use the **at** command to run several command lines at a specified time. In this case, press **Enter** at the end of each command line, and then press **Ctrl-D** when you're finished entering command lines.

When you're through entering command lines, the **at** command will display a job-ID, confirming that the job will run at a certain time. To see a list of pending job generated with the **at** command, use the following command line:

```
$ at -1
```

To remove a job scheduled with the **at** command, you'll need to get the job-ID (as listed with the *–1* option) and then use the *–r* option to **at**:

```
$ at -r job-ID
```

where *job-ID* refers to the ID number returned by the *–1* option.

The Command Reference for the **at** command is listed in Table 5.11. As you can tell, the **at** command can sometimes be very involved.

TABLE 5.11   THE COMMAND REFERENCE FOR THE AT COMMAND.

at option1 *time [date] increment*
at option2 *[job-id]*

Purpose
The **at** command performs specified commands at given times and dates, as long as the commands require no additional input from you.

There are two of sets of options available with the **at** commands. One set of options, *option1*, relates to setting the targeted time and date. The second set of options, *option2*, allows changes to jobs already scheduled.

After you enter the **at** command, you type in the commands to execute at that time. You type in these commands at the keyboard. When you're finished, press **Ctrl-D**.

At the given time, **at** runs your commands. Any output from the commands is sent to you via electronic mail.

Options Relating to Scheduling

–f *filename*	Executes the commands listed in *filename*, rather than the commands input from the keyboard. (Not available on all systems.)
–m	Notifies user when job is completed via electronic mail, instead of the default of informing via a message on the screen. *continued*

Time Options

time	The time when the commands should run. Unless you specify otherwise (with am or pm as a suffix), the system assumes military time.
midnight **noon** **now**	These options are used in lieu of a specific time. If you use **now** as an option, you must specify an increment (see below).

Date Options

date	Format is usually specified as *month, day, year,* with year optional.
day	The specific day when the command should run, with the name either spelled out (*Sunday*) or referred to by the first three letters (*Sun*).
today **tomorrow**	These options are used in lieu of a specific date.

Options Relating to Already-Scheduled Jobs

−l	Lists current job.
−r	Removes specified job.

Increment Options

increment	A numerical value relative to the current time and date. The increment must contain a reference to **minute**, **hour**, **day**, **week**, **month**, or **year**. In the case of *at now + 2 weeks)*, the job would be performed two weeks from now.

The Batch Command

Similar to the **at** command is the **batch** command.

Instead of running through a series of command lines *at* a specified time, the **batch** command runs through a series of command lines immediately. These command lines are run in the background, which means the system doesn't put a particularly high priority on them. Again, this command is useful when you're performing some basic chores and aren't in a hurry to complete them.

Using the **batch** command is a matter of the following command line:

```
$ batch
```

As with the **at** command, the cursor appears on the following line *sans* prompt, letting you know that the **batch** command is waiting for input. Enter your command lines, ending each with the **Return** key (or the **Enter** key, depending on your system). When you're through entering command lines, type **Ctrl-D.**

The **batch** command will then run the commands in the order that they were entered into the system. You'll receive no feedback from the system as commands are executed; instead, you'll be sent a mail message telling you that the command is complete (or, if the command requires some feedback sent to you, you'll receive this feedback also via mail). In addition, the **batch** command makes sure that each command line is finished, even if the system goes down.

The command is summarized in Table 5.12.

TABLE 5.12 COMMAND REFERENCE FOR THE BATCH COMMAND.

batch

Purpose

The **batch** command runs a series of commands one command at a time in the background.

Options

None.

The Nohup Command

If you begin a task and aren't sure if it will be completed before you hit Happy Hour, you may want to use it in conjunction with the **nohup** command.

The **nohup** (which stands for *no hangup*) command tells the command line to continue running even after you log off the system. A typical **nohup** command line looks like the following:

$ nohup *command arguments filename(s)* &

where *command* is the name of the command you want to run, *arguments* refers to the arguments for the *command* (*not* for **nohup**) and the *filename(s)* used as input for the command. In addition, you'll probably want to run the **nohup** command in the background.

There's really not too much more to the **nohup** command, as you'll see from Table 5.13.

TABLE 5.13 COMMAND REFERENCE FOR THE NOHUP COMMAND.

nohup *command arguments* &

Purpose

The **nohup** keeps a command running even if you log off the system.

Options

None.

This Chapter in Review

▲ One of the prime reasons companies go for the UNIX operating system is its ability to support multiple users in a variety of ways.

▲ Because of this support, you'll find that a typical computing session on a UNIX system is a lot different than on a PC running DOS. For starters, you need to login a UNIX system, entering your username and your password.

▲ Your password is a sacred and precious object. Misuse of it could lead to some serious breaches in system security. Guard your password with your life.

▲ When you login a system, there are files stored in your home directory that will shape your UNIX system usage.

While it's too early in your UNIX experience to be editing these files, you can change some of the things that these files set.

▲ The shell also oversees standard input/output on a UNIX system. While DOS supports standard input/output and related tools like redirection and pipes, most DOS usage doesn't require knowledge of the subject. However, UNIX usage stresses the practice.

▲ UNIX also features the ability to run more than task at one time; as you might expect, this capability is called multitasking. To run a command in the background, end the command line with an ampersand (**&**). To track which tasks are running, use the **ps** command.

▲ There are several UNIX commands that rely on the ability to run more than one task at a given time, including **at** and **nohup**.

▪ CHAPTER SIX ▪
Basic UNIX Tools

The UNIX operating system features a host of tools—some with direct counterparts in the DOS world, and some unique to UNIX—that work on files and directories and can in general make your life easier. These tools include:

▲ The **cat** command, which can be used in a wide variety of situations

▲ The **more** command, which is used for viewing files

▲ The **pg** command, which is used for viewing files

▲ The **head** command, which is used for viewing the first 10 lines of a file

▲ The **tail** command, which is used for viewing the last 10 lines of a file

▲ The **find** command, which is to track down errant files

▲ The **sort** command, which is used to sort files

▲ The **comm** command, which is used to compare files

▲ The **cmp** command, which is used to compare files

▲ The **diff** command, which is used to compare files

▲ The **bdiff** command, which is used to compare files

▲ The **sdiff** command, which is used to compare files

More Commands About Files and Directories

You didn't really think that Chapter 4 said everything there was to say about commands relating to files and directories, did you? The vast majority of commands in UNIX—and DOS, for that matter—have to do with the usage of files and directories in some manner. Chapter 4 was a sampler of *direct* file/directory commands. This chapter extends that discussion with a review of commands that *do* things to files and directories. A fine distinction, perhaps—but you wouldn't want to be overwhelmed by UNIX commands in one shot, would you?

The Cat Command

Considering how specialized most UNIX commands are, the existence of the **cat** command is quite a surprise.

In many ways, the **cat** command is the Swiss Army knives of UNIX commands. You can use it to view a file. You can use it to combine files. You can use it to edit files. And you can use it to create a file. The **cat** command is summarized in Table 6.1, and as you progress through this chapter, you'll probably want to review this summary often.

TABLE 6.1 COMMAND REFERENCE FOR THE CAT COMMAND.

> **cat** *options file(s)*
>
> **Purpose**
>
> The **cat** command performs several frequently used chores:
>
> ▲ Combines several files into a new file (using the > operator).
>
> ▲ Appends other files to an existing file (using the >> operator).
>
> *continued*

▲   Displays a file when no operators are specified.

▲   Copies a file to a new name (using the > operator).

▲   Creates a new text file without the use of a text editor.

Options

−   Used as a substitute for a filename, − allows for keyboard entry to be appended to an existing file. **Ctrl-D** to end the keyboard entry.

−s   Silent mode; suppresses information about nonexistent files.

−u   Output is unbuffered; default is buffered, which means that characters are displayed in blocks.

−v   Prints nonprinting characters, such as control characters, except for tabs, form feeds, and newlines.

−ve   Prints nonprinting characters, such as control characters, except for tabs and forms feeds, while newlines appear as dollar signs ($).

−vt   Prints nonprinting characters, such as control characters, except for newlines, while tabs appear as ^I and form feeds as ^L.

−vet Print all nonprinting characters.

There's no counterpart to **cat** in the DOS world, so no comparisons can be made for you. However, the **cat** command is so important and useful that it warrants coverage on its own, irrespective of any DOS-analogy situations.

Using Cat to View Files

The first situation where you'll find **cat** useful is in something very basic: viewing files. On this level, **cat** is quite simple. To display a file on the screen, you merely combine **cat** with the filename on a command line. To display the file **kevin.report**, you'd use the following command line:

```
$ cat kevin.report
```

You can display more than one file at a time, one after another. To display **kevin.report**, followed by **kevin.memo**, you'd use the following command line:

```
$ cat kevin.report kevin.memo
```

If you enter **cat** on a command line and fail to specify a file, you'll be frustrated to find that no matter what you typed, your keystrokes would merely be displayed on the screen. One of the uses for **cat** involves creating a file from scratch. When you use **cat** without a filename, you're invoking this usage. To end this charade, use **Ctrl-D** to end input.

If you're viewing a longer file with the **cat** command, you may find that the text whizzes by on the screen at an uncomfortably fast rate—fast enough so that you won't be able to read it. Because there's no way to control how **cat** displays text, it's best used with shorter files that don't run longer than a screen when displayed.

Using Cat to Copy Files

You can use **cat** to create a new file that has the contents of an existing file, essentially as a substitute for the **cp** command (which you learned about in Chapter 4). You must specify both the original and new file on the command line, separated by a > symbol. The command line for saving the contents of the file **thea** into a new file named **geisha** would look like this:

```
$ cat thea > geisha
```

The file **thea** would be unchanged.

Using Cat to Combine Files

Cat's original purpose was a tool for combining files—**cat** is actually short for *concatenate*—and it still can be used for that purpose.

However, using **cat** for this purpose is probably a little trickier than you might expect, so this usage will be explained though a series of examples. Let's say you wanted to combine the files **thea** and **geisha** into a new file named **spike**. The following command line does just that:

```
$ cat thea geisha > spike
```

The order of the files of the command line determine the content of the new file. In this instance, the contents of the file **thea** would be followed by the contents of the file **geisha**. Again, the contents of the files **thea** and **geisha** would be unchanged.

Using Cat to Edit Text

You can also use **cat** as a rudimentary text editor. If you want to open a file named **cats** and then type in its contents, you'd use the following command line:

```
$ cat > cats
```

All subsequent keyboard input would be stored in the new file named **cats**. When you're done typing into this new file, there are a few things you'll need to note:

▲ You must press the **Enter** key at the end of every line. If you don't, **cat** will refuse to accept more keystrokes.

▲ You can make changes with the **Backspace** key, moving back as you type. However, you can't perform any other movements via the scroll keys.

▲ When you're finished typing into the file, type **Ctrl-D** to end input.

Using Cat to Append Data

You can use **cat** to append data to an existing file. The following command line places the contents of the file **thea** into an existing file named **spike**:

```
$ cat thea >> spike
```

If you want to add to a file (in this case, a file named **geisha**) directly from your keyboard, you can do so with the following command line:

```
$ cat - >> geisha
```

If you're not careful about how you use the **cat** command, you could easily overwrite the contents of one file with keyboard entry or the contents of another file. For instance, the command:

```
    $ cat - > spike
```

replaces the current contents of the file **spike** with keyboard input. **Cat** will not warn you when you're making changes to existing files, so you need to be *very* careful when using this command.

Looking at Files with More And Pg

Using **cat** to view files is OK when the file is not on the smaller side. However, when files are on the larger side, there are a few UNIX commands more suited to the task: **more** and **pg**.

The UNIX commands should be somewhat familiar to you; the DOS command **MORE** works pretty much like the UNIX **more** and **pg** commands. However, the *way* each command is used on a command line differs.

The DOS **MORE** command uses a rather unusual—unusual for a DOS command, anyway—syntax for displaying a file. The logical use of the **MORE** command would be to use it with the name of the file you want to display:

```
C:\WINDOWS> MORE BOOTLOG.TXT
    Too many arguments in command line
```

Instead, you must use a redirection command (<) to tell **MORE** where to get the input for the command (in this case, the input is the file you want to view), as in the following command line:

```
C:\WINDOWS> MORE < BOOTLOG.TXT
```

This command yields a response as shown in Figure 6.1: The contents of the file **BOOTLOG.TXT**.

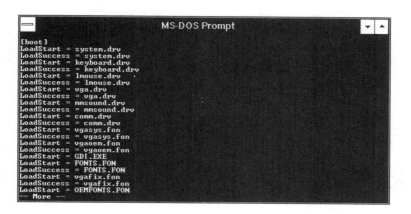

```
[boot]
LoadStart = system.drv
LoadSuccess = system.drv
LoadStart = keyboard.drv
LoadSuccess = keyboard.drv
LoadStart = lmouse.drv    .
LoadSuccess = lmouse.drv
LoadStart = vga.drv
LoadSuccess = vga.drv
LoadStart = mmsound.drv
LoadSuccess = mmsound.drv
LoadStart = comm.drv
LoadSuccess = comm.drv
LoadStart = vgasys.fon
LoadSuccess = vgasys.fon
LoadStart = vgaoem.fon
LoadSuccess = vgaoem.fon
LoadStart = GDI.EXE
LoadStart = FONTS.FON
LoadSuccess = FONTS.FON
LoadStart = vgafix.fon
LoadSuccess = vgafix.fon
LoadStart = OEMFONTS.FON
-- More --
```

FIGURE 6.1 The DOS MORE command in action.

For longer files, you should use **more** or **pg** to display the files. The **more** command will display a file one screen at a time. It also is more interactive than the **cat** command, in that **more** tells you how much of the file is left to view, and it will also allow you to go back to screens you'd previously viewed, as well as specify a starting line number for viewing a file. Using the **more** command to read a file named **kevin.file** is a matter of putting together a simple command line:

```
$ more kevin.file
```

However, you'll find that the **more** command is made more useful by invoking the *–d* option, which places short instructions on the bottom of the screen (*very* short instructions—**Enter** to continue, **Delete** key to end). A command line using this option would look like:

```
$ more -d kevin.file
```

The full list of options associated with the **more** command are listed in the command's Command Reference, found in Table 6.2.

TABLE 6.2 COMMAND REFERENCE FOR THE MORE COMMAND.

more *options file(s)*

Purpose

The **more** command displays all or parts of a file one screenful at a time. Type **q** to quit, space bar to continue.

Options

–c	Clears the screen before displaying the next page of the file. This can be quicker than watching pages scroll by.
–d	Displays a prompt at the bottom of the screen, involving brief instructions.
–f	Wraps text to fit the screen width and judge the page length accordingly.
–l	Ignores formfeeds (^L) at the end of a page.
–r	Displays control characters. (Not available on all systems.)
–s	Squeeze; ignores multiple blank lines.
–u	Ignores formatting characteristics like underlined text.
–w	Waits for user input for exiting.
–n	Sets window size by *n* lines.
+num	Starts output at line number *num*.

Options When Viewing a File

f	Go to next full screen.
n	Display next file.
p	Display previous file.
q	Quit.

There's only one problem with the **more** command: It's not available on every UNIX system. However, almost every UNIX system does have a similar command called **pg**, which displays a file one page at a time. (The command also goes by the name **page** on some systems; **pg** and **page** are for the most part interchangeable command names.) As you can tell by the Command Reference for **pg** (found in Table 6.3), there are many similarities between **more** and **pg**. However, **more** is a little easier to use than **pg** for beginners.

To use **pg** to view a file named **spike.file**, you'd use the following command line:

```
$ pg spike.file
```

If this file was longer than one screen, you'll see a colon (**:**) on the bottom of the screen. This is where you'd enter a command (as listed in Table 6.3), or else you can hit the **Return** key to go to the next screen.

There are a number of useful commands associated with the **pg** command when the color (**:**) prompt is displayed:

▲ To move ahead to the next page, press the **Enter** or **Return** key.

▲ To move back one page, press the – (hyphen) key, then the **Enter** key.

▲ To move ahead a specific number of pages, press the **+** (plus) key, followed by the number of pages you want to move ahead, then the **Enter** key.

▲ To move back a specific number of pages, press the – (minus) key followed by the number of pages you want to move back, then the **Enter** key.

▲ To move forward a specific number of lines, press the **+** (plus) key, then the number of lines you want to move ahead, then the letter *l* (short for lines), then the **Enter** key.

▲ To move back a specific number of lines, press the – (minus) key, then the number of lines you want to move back, then the letter *l* (short for lines), then the **Enter** key.

▲ To move ahead by a half-page, press the letter *d*, then the **Enter** key.

▲ To move to a specific string, enter the string between two slashes (*/string/*), then press the **Enter** key.

TABLE 6.3 COMMAND REFERENCE FOR THE PG COMMAND.

pg *options file(s)*

Purpose

The **pg** command displays all or parts of a file. Type **q** to quit, space bar to continue.

Options

–c   Clears the screen before displaying the next page of the file. This can be quicker than watching pages scroll by.

–n   Sets window size by *n* lines.

Commands During File Viewing

l   Move ahead or back as measured by lines.

n   Display next file.

p   Display previous file.

q   Quit.

Head and Tail

There are times when you'll want to look at only the beginning or end of a file, in cases where you want to make sure that a given file contains certain data. In these cases, the commands **head** and **tail** allows you to view just the beginnings and ends of files.

To look at the first ten lines of a file, use the **head** command:

```
$ head file
```

where *file* is the name of the file you want to view.

To look at the last ten lines of a file, use the **tail** file:

```
$ tail file
```

where *file* is the name of the file you want to view.

You can combine both commands with a numeral, if you don't want to view ten lines. For instance, to view the first 20 lines of a file with the **head** command, you'd use the following command line:

```
$ head -20 file
```

where *file* is the name of the file you want to view. Similarly, the following command line would display the last 20 lines of a file:

```
$ tail -20 file
```

where *file* is the name of the file you want to view.

The **head** command is summarized in Table 6.4, while the **tail** command is summarized in Table 6.5.

TABLE 6.4 COMMAND REFERENCE FOR THE HEAD COMMAND.

head *option file(s)*

Purpose

The **head** command displays the beginning of a file. The default is 10 lines.

Options

–*n*   Specifies the number of lines to display. The default is 10 lines.

TABLE 6.5 COMMAND REFERENCE FOR THE TAIL COMMAND.

tail *options file*

Purpose

The **tail** command displays the final 10 lines of a file. However, vendors change the specifics of this command; both HP-UX and Solaris treat this command differently from the options listed here.

Options

–f   "Follows" growth of file should changes be made while **tail** command is active. Use **Ctrl-D** to stop the process.

–r   Displays lines in reverse order. Not available on all systems.

–*n*b Displays the last *n* blocks.

+*n*b Displays all blocks after block *n*.

–*n*c Displays the last *n* characters.

+*n*c Displays all characters after *n*.

–*n*l Displays the last *n* lines.

+*n*l Display all lines after line *n*.

Finding Files with Find

The DOS command **FIND** has a limited usefulness: You use it to search for a text string within a specific file. While there are times when this approach can be useful, a more useful route for a command named **find** would concern finding a filename. Then again, because DOS wasn't built to work with large numbers of files, there wasn't a heavy need for a command that would find a file.

A more workable alternative for *Windows* users lies within the *Windows* File Manager. The **Search** menu item under the File Menu will look for a file anywhere on your system, as shown in Figure 6.2.

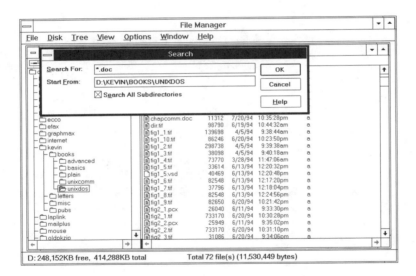

FIGURE 6.2 The Search command.

However, the need to track down files existed in UNIX from the beginning; hence the **find** command. The **find** command will ferret its way through your filesystem and find a specified file or files. You can use it to look for one specific file, or you can use wildcards and a whole other host of options to specify a range of files. You can look for all files ending with the string *.w*. You can look for all files that were created within the last three days. And so on.

Because of such a wide range of abilities and an extremely odd syntax, **find** is probably more difficult to use than it should be. Take, for example, the basic command itself as part of a command line. You would think that it would be easy to look for a file named **report** as part of a command line like the following:

```
$ find report
```

If you run this command line, you'll do nothing but generate an error command from the system, since **find** doesn't work like any other command in the UNIX universe. Instead, you must tell **find** that you want to look for a file by name, and then you must tell it that you actually want to see the output of the command on the screen (this lack of adherence to UNIX standard input/output, which you learned about in Chapter 5, is remarkably aberrant). If you don't tell **find** that you actually want to see the results the search, **find** will complete the search without telling you.

Therefore, to find a file named **report**, you'd need to use a command line like this:

```
$ find / -name 'report' -print
```

Three distinct elements are present in this command line:

▲ /, which tells the **find** command to look through the entire filesystem

▲ *–name*, which tells **find** to search for a file by name

▲ *'report'*, which tells **find** to look for a filename specifically named **report**

▲ *–print*, which tells **find** to print the results of the search to the screen

This command isn't recommended for anyone working on a large UNIX system. When you tell **find** to work through *every* directory, it will do just that. You could spend a lot of time twiddling your thumbs while waiting for this command to complete. And there's the very likely chance that on a larger system more than one user will have used the not-exactly-uncommon filename of **report**.

Therefore, it's best to limit your searches to a specific portion of the UNIX filesystem, or to introduce other limiting factors that are supported by **find** options. For instance, you may know that you last read the file **report** three days ago. Armed with this knowledge, you can tell **find** to find a file named **report** that was accessed three days ago, as follows:

```
$ find / -name 'report' -ctime 3 -print
```

There are a ton of options to **find**, thankfully. They are listed in Table 6.6.

TABLE 6.6 COMMAND REFERENCE FOR THE FIND COMMAND.

find *pathname(s) condition(s)*

Purpose

Finds a file. Of course, it's not *quite* that simple—you enter as many conditions as you want (relating to when the file was created, when it was last accessed, what links are present, and so on, as you'll see when you review the available conditions).

Options

–atime *days*	Finds files that were accessed:
	+d more than *d* days ago.
	d exactly *d* days ago.
	–d fewer than *d* days ago.
–ctime *days*	Finds files that were changed:
	+d more than *d* days ago.
	d exactly *d* days ago.
	–d fewer than *d* days ago.
–exec *command* { } \;	Runs UNIX *command* after a file is found.
–follow	Follows symbolic links and the associated directories.
–fstype *type*	Finds files of a specific filesystem *type*.
–group *group*	Finds files belonging to group *group*, which can be a name or ID.

continued

–inum *num*	Finds a file with an inode number of *num*.
–links *links*	Finds files with:
	+*l* more than *l* links.
	l exactly *l* links.
	-*l* fewer than *l* links.
–local	Search for files on the local file-system. (Not available on all systems.)
–mtime *days*	Finds files that were modified:
	+*d* more than *d* days ago.
	d exactly *d* days ago.
	–*d* fewer than *d* days ago.
–name *file*	Finds a file named *file*.
–newer *filename*	Returns all files that have been modified more recently than *filename*.
–nogroup	Find files owned by a group not listed in **/etc/group**.
–nouser	Find files owned by a user not listed in **/etc/passwd**.
–ok *command* { } \;	Runs UNIX *command* after a file is found, verifying the action with the user.
–perms *nnn*	Matches specified file permissions (such as **rwx**).
–print	Prints the results of the search to the screen. This option is mandatory, if you want to see the results of your search.
–size *blocks* [chars]	Find a file that is *blocks* blocks large, or *chars* characters large.

continued

–type *t*	Returns names of files of type *t*. Type *t* can be **b** (block special file), **c** (character special file), **d** (directory), **f** (plain file), **l** (symbolic link), or **p** (pipe).
–user *user*	Matches files belonging to a user, specified by name or ID.
–xdev	Search for files on the same file system as the specified *pathname*. (Only for BSD systems.)
Logical Selectors	
–a	and
–o	or
\!	not
\(...\)	group together

Using Find in the Background

You could run this command in the background and then redirect the output to a file. As you'll recall from Chapter 5, running a command in the background means that you can perform other tasks while the command goes on its merry way. Redirecting the results of the command to a file means that instead of being displayed on the screen, the results will be stored in a file. The following command would run **find** in the background (as indicated by the trailing ampersand) and then send the results to a file named **results**:

```
$ find / -name 'report' -print > results &
```

Sorting Files with Sort

UNIX tends to be a fussy operating system. When it comes to organizing data, UNIX loves to have things just so, which you'll find as you use some of the more advanced UNIX commands. That's why there are several commands that can be used to organize the contents of files. Chief among these commands is the **sort** command.

Even though there's a DOS command named **SORT**, you're probably not familiar with it: This particular command is hard to use, and the limited sorting it can accomplish can be done more easily by other tools. So this section will assume that you know nothing about the DOS **SORT** command—which means you'll need a complete introduction to the UNIX **sort** command.

The easiest way to learn how the **sort** command works is to see it in action. As a frivolous example: You're a baseball fan, and you've entered the teams in the American League Central in a file called **AL_Central**. You've not really paid much attention to the order when you created the file, so the file looks something like this (as seen with the **cat** command):

```
$ cat AL_Central
Minnesota
Milwaukee
Chicago
Cleveland
Kansas City
```

Being from Chicago, you don't like the fact that *Minnesota* leads off the file, so you decide to put *Chicago* in its rightful alphabetical spot on the top of the file. The **sort** command changes the alphabetical order of lines within a file, so you decide to use it on your **AL_Central** file:

```
$ sort AL_Central
Chicago
Cleveland
Kansas City
Milwaukee
Minnesota
```

However, your original file will remain unchanged, as the **sort** command writes its standard output to the screen, not to a file or a printer. If you wanted your **AL_Central** file to reflect changes made by the **sort** command, you'll have to redirect the output to a file, as you learned about in Chapter 2. (If you're still a little fuzzy about standard input/output and redirection, a review of Chapter 5 is definitely in order.) To direct the results of the **sort** command to a new file named **AL_Cen.sort**, you'd use the following command line:

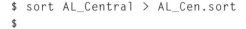
```
$ sort AL_Central > AL_Cen.sort
$
```

(The use of the *sort* suffix here is purely arbitrary and not the direct result of using the **sort** command. However, when you're keeping track of many files, a good way to tell them apart is to place a distinctive suffix onto files, especially one linked to the steps used to create them. This practice will be used throughout this chapter.)

Because you've redirected the results of the **sort** command to a file, nothing appears on the screen. However, if you were to view the contents of the new file named **AL_Cen.sort**, you'd see the following:

```
$ cat AL_Cen.sort
Chicago
Cleveland
Kansas City
Milwaukee
Minnesota
```

If you were to try and write the results of the **sort** command to the same filename, the system would generate an error message. This safeguard exists so that beginning users like yourself don't accidentally sort a file and make the changes permanent. (In fact, it's a good idea to *always* view the results of a sort on the screen before committing them to a file.) However, there obviously are times when you do want to overwrite an existing file. In this situation, you're not using the UNIX redirection procedure, but rather an option associated with the **sort** command, *–o*:

```
$ sort -o AL_Central AL_Central
```

Other options are listed in Table 6.7.

TABLE 6.7 COMMAND REFERENCE FOR THE SORT COMMAND.

> **sort** *options files*
>
> **Purpose**
>
> The **sort** command sorts the lines of files, usually in alphabetical order. Commands like **comm** and **join** require sorted files in order to work, which is the real reason for the existence of **sort**—not to arrange baseball standings.   *continued*

166

▼

Options

–b	Ignores leading spaces and tabs.
–c	Checks if *files* are already sorted. If they are, **sort** does nothing.
–d	Sorts in dictionary order (ignore punctuation).
–f	Ignores the case of the sort entries.
–i	Ignores non-ASCII characters when sorting.
–m	Merges files that have already been sorted.
–M	Sorts the files assuming the first three characters are months.
–n	Sorts in numeric order.
–o*file*	Stores output in *file*. The default is to send output to standard output.
–r	Reverses the order of the sort—starting either with the end of the alphabet or the largest numeral.
–z*n*	Provides a maximum of *n* characters per line of input.
+*n*[–*m*]	Skips *n* fields before sorting, and then sorts through line *m*.

The **sort** command can be used to sort multiple files. To combine and alphabetize the entire American League, you'd use the following:

```
$ sort AL_West AL_Central AL_East
Baltimore
Boston
California
Chicago
Cleveland
Detroit
Kansas City
Milwaukee
Minnesota
New York
Oakland
```

```
Seattle
Texas
Toronto
$
```

Redirection also can be used with multiple files:

```
$ sort AL_West AL_Central AL_East > American
$
```

Not every sort you need is going to be alphabetical, however—many will be numerical in nature. For instance, if you're maintaining the standings of the American League Central (complete with wins and losses), you'll want to do sorts on a numerical rather than an alphabetical basis. To sort a file by numeral, use the *–n* options:

```
$ sort -n AL_Central
```

Here's what the resulting file would look like after such a sort:

```
$ sort -n AL_Central
10 50 Milwaukee
20 40 Kansas City
30 30 Cleveland
40 20 Chicago
49 11 Minnesota
```

The three columns seen above are referred to as *fields* in UNIX parlance. For the **sort** command to work, each of the lines must be consistent in the number of fields within the lines, and also in the organization of the fields.

For what we want to do, the *–n* option takes us only part of the way. In this situation, we want to sort the files in reverse order, showing that the team with the most wins is at the top of the standings. In this case, you'd want to use the *–r* option in conjunction with the *–n* option:

```
$ sort -rn AL_Central
49 11 Minnesota
40 20 Chicago
30 30 Cleveland
20 40 Kansas City
10 50 Milwaukee
```

The **sort** command can also be used to sort based on a specific column, not necessarily the beginning of the line, as shown in the following two examples:

```
$ sort +1 AL_Central
49 11 Minnesota
40 20 Chicago
30 30 Cleveland
20 40 Kansas City
10 50 Milwaukee

$ sort +2 AL_Central
40 20 Chicago
30 30 Cleveland
20 40 Kansas City
10 50 Milwaukee
49 11 Minnesota
```

There's no limit to the number of columns you can skip when using the +*n* option (where *n* refers to the number of columns to be skipped).

Reality Check: Using Sort

For some reason or another, beginners tend to have a tough time with the **sort** command. Often, they'll use **sort** and find that the data returned by **sort** isn't what they expected.

There's one simple reason for this: They are using **sort** on a file that isn't formatted consistently. When using the –*r* and –*n* options, for instance, beginners will throw in a few lines that don't begin with numerals. Or, when using the +*n* option, they'll have three columns in one line, four in another, and two in a third line—but then they expect **sort** to know which column to sort.

Always remember: UNIX is a fussy and precise operating system. It will do *exactly* as you tell it. And since there's often not a lot of interaction associated with UNIX commands, you need to make sure that all elements of the command line are precise.

File Comparisons With Comm and Cmp

The DOS **COMP** command died a death with the release of MS-DOS 6.0, and with good reason: It was an example of a good idea wrapped up in terrible execution. The **COMP** file compared two files and then could be made to list the first 10 instances where the files differed. Unfortunately, the output from this command was obscure, and essentially all it was good for was to see if two files were truly different.

A better DOS effort is **FC**, which compares two files and then lists the lines that differ.

UNIX also includes several tools for comparing files. This capability is probably more important in the UNIX world, as a UNIX system simply deals with a much larger volume of files than does the average DOS system.

One of the most commonly used UNIX tools is **comm**, which is used to compare sorted files. Why sorted files? Because **comm** does line-by-line comparisons. If the files aren't similar in order and structure, the results of the **comm** command aren't going to mean much.

However, there's one huge drawback to the **comm** command: It works only on text files—and sorted text files, to boot. It won't work with any program files, nor will it work with any specially formatted files that are created by applications like *AutoCAD* or *FrameMaker*.

Keeping with the baseball motif: Let's say you wanted to compare the contents of the **American** file with the contents of the **National** file. You've already sorted both files, so the entries are in alphabetical order. The resulting command line and output would look like this:

```
$ comm American National
                Atlanta
Baltimore
Boston
California
                                        Chicago
        Cincinnati
```

```
Cleveland
                    Colorado
Detroit
                    Florida
                    Houston
Kansas City
                    Los Angeles
Milwaukee
Minnesota
                    Montreal
                                        New York
Oakland
                    Philadelphia
                    Pittsburgh
                    San Diego
                    San Francisco
Seattle
                    St. Louis
Texas
Toronto
```

The output is organized in three columns: Column 1 lists lines unique to the first file listed on the command line (in this case, **American**), Column 2 lists lines unique to the second file listed on the command line (in this case, **National**), and Column 3 lists lines occurring in both files.

Like all UNIX commands, you can save the results of the **comm** command into a file using redirection. In this case, you're saving the results of the above **comm** command into a file called **baseball.sort**:

```
$ comm American National > baseball.sort
```

Perhaps more useful in most situations, though not this specific example, is the –*u* option to **comm**, which compares two files and eliminates redundancies:

```
$ comm -u American National > baseball.comm
```

This command saves the comparison done by **comm** to the file **baseball.comm**, with only one *Chicago* line and one *New Yor*k line. Other options to the **comm** command are listed in Table 6.8.

The *–u* option isn't supported on some older UNIX systems, though it is included in System V Release 4.

TABLE 6.8 COMMAND REFERENCE FOR THE COMM COMMAND.

comm *options file1 file2*

Purpose

The **comm** command compares the contents of two presorted text files. The output is generated in three columns:

Lines found	Lines found	Lines found
in *file1*	in *file2*	in both files

Options

–1	Suppresses the printing of column 1.
–2	Suppresses the printing of column 2.
–3	Suppresses the printing of column 3.
–12	Prints only column 3.
–13	Prints only column 2.
–23	Prints only column 1.

Of course, there are other commands used to compare files. One of the simplest of such commands is the **cmp** command, which tells you if two files are different; if they are, **cmp** prints out the first line that is different in the two files. Again, this command helps you to better manage the multitude of files that you'll create throughout your normal work.

After looking through two files with the **cat** command, you'll see how the **cmp** command works:

```
$ cat brady.1993
Dear Brady:
It's time for another hokey television
reunion! As you know, this year's theme
is to be how Marcia has dealt with
the loss of a loved one. I'm sure you'll
agree that we have another hit on our
hands! I look forward to seeing you on
March 12, 1993.
--Your producer

$ cat brady.1994
Dear Brady:
It's time for another hokey television
reunion! As you know, this year's theme
is to be how Greg has dealt with
the loss of a loved one. I'm sure you'll
agree that we have another hit on our
hands! I look forward to seeing you on
April 16, 1994.
--Your producer

$ cmp brady.1993 brady.1994
brady.1993 brady.1994 differ: char 14, line 4
```

The **cmp** command reports that the first difference between **brady.1993** and **brady.1994** occurs in the fourth line, in the 14th character. This is *all* the **cmp** command will tell you—you won't know to what extent the files differ, nor will you know other specific instances where the files differ. There are a few options of dubious worth, as listed in Table 6.9.

TABLE 6.9 COMMAND REFERENCE FOR THE CMP COMMAND.

cmp *options file1 file2*

Purpose

The **cmp** command compares the contents of two files. If the files are different, **cmp** returns the byte position and line number of the first difference between the two files. If there is no difference in the files, then **cmp** returns nothing. The **cmp** command works on all files, not just text files. Similar commands, such as **diff** and **comm**, work only with text files.

Options

–l   Displays the byte position and the differing characters for all differences within the file.

–s   Works silently, returning only the exit codes and not the instances of differences. The exit code is one of the following:

   0   Files are identical.

   1   Files are different.

   2   One of the files is unreadable.

Using diff to Discover More Information

For more extensive information, you'll want to use the **diff** command.

The **diff** command first reports if the files are different, and then lists each instance where the files differ. Using the two previous files as examples, you can see how **diff** works:

```
$ diff brady.1993 brady.1994
4c4
< is to be how Marcia has dealt with
- - -
> is to be how Greg has dealt with
8c8
< March 12, 1993.
- - -
> April 16, 1994.
```

Even on short files with only nine lines, **diff** reports a lot of information. Lines beginning with the < symbol occur in the first file listed on the command line, while lines beginning with the > symbol occur within the second file listed on the command line. The dashed line separates the two lines. The numerals refer to the specific lines that differ.

The Command Reference for the **diff** command can be found in Table 6.10.

TABLE 6.10 COMMAND REFERENCE FOR THE DIFF COMMAND.

diff *options diroptions file1 file2*
Purpose

The **diff** command compares two files and reports differing lines. The line numbers of the differing lines are noted, while the unique line from *file1* is marked with <, and the unique line from *file2* is marked with >. Three hyphens (– – –) separate the contents of the two files. This command works best with text files.

Options

–b　Ignores blanks at the end of line.

–i　Ignores case.

–t　Expands tabs in output to spaces.

–w　Ignores spaces and tabs.

There are many variations on **diff** within the various versions of UNIX, each slightly different than the main **diff** command. **Bdiff**, for example, works best with long files, while the **diff3** is used to compare three files (though, as you'll see by the options listed in Table 6.11, it works best as a front end for a text editor named **ed**, which you'll learn about in Chapter 8). And the ever-popular **sdiff** command reports which lines are the same and which are different.

The Command Reference for **bdiff** can be found in Table 6.11. The Command Reference for **diff3** can be found in Table 6.12. And the Command Reference for **sdiff** can be found in Table 6.13.

TABLE 6.11 COMMAND REFERENCE FOR THE BDIFF COMMAND.

bdiff *file1 file2 options*

Purpose

The **bdiff** command compares two files and reports on the differing lines. This command invokes the **diff** command after dividing a file into manageable chunks—thus making it more suitable than **diff** when it comes to larger files—and it works best with text files.

Options

n   Divides the files into segments *n* lines long.

−s   Suppresses error messages.

TABLE 6.12 COMMAND REFERENCE FOR THE DIFF3 COMMAND.

diff3 *options file1 file2 file3*

Purpose

The **diff3** command compares three different files and reports the differences. This command returns one of the following codes:

  ====   All three files differ.

  ====1 *file1* is different.

  ====2 *file2* is different.

  ====3 *file3* is different.

Options

−e   Creates an **ed** script that places differences between *file2* and *file3* into *file1*. Not available on all systems.

−E   Creates an **ed** script that places differences between *file2* and *file3* into *file1*, marking lines that differ in all three files with brackets.

−x   Creates an **ed** script that places differences between all three files.

−X   Creates an **ed** script that places differences between all three files, marking lines that differ in all three files with brackets. Not available on all systems.

−3   Creates an **ed** script that places differences between *file1* and *file3* into *file1*.

TABLE 6.13 COMMAND REFERENCE FOR THE SDIFF COMMAND.

sdiff *options file1 file2*

Purpose

The **sdiff** command compares *file1* with *file2* and reports on the differences, as well as identical lines. Output occurs in four forms:

text text	lines are identical.
text <	line exists only in *file1*.
text >	line exists only in *file2*.
*text	text*	lines are different.

Options

–l	Reports only on lines that are identical in *file1*.
–o *file*	Sends identical lines to *file*.
–s	Does not return identical lines.

This Chapter in Review

▲   There are a number of extended UNIX commands that you'll use often in your UNIX computing experience. Some of them have counterparts in the DOS world, while others are unique to UNIX.

▲   The handiest UNIX command is **cat**, which can perform a variety of functions. The most common function, perhaps, is for viewing a file without having to invoke a text editor.

▲   Cat can also be used to combine files (thanks to some redirection on the command line) and copy files. Yet another usage is appending data to the end of existing files.

▲   Also used for viewing files—especially longer files—are **more** and **pg**. **More** may be easier to use, but **pg** offers more options and maneuverability when viewing files. The commands **head** and **tail** can be used to view the beginning and end of files, respectively.

▲   UNIX likes structure. As a result, there are times when you'll want to rearrange the contents of a file for some streamline database management. The powerful **sort** command will sort a file to your specifications.

▲ UNIX features a number of commands used to compare files, continuing the emphasis on UNIX's prime role as a file manager. Two of the most common commands for this purpose are **comm** and **cmp**.

▲ The members of the **diff** family can also be used to compare files. Depending on your needs, you could made use of **diff**, **bdiff**, or **sdiff**.

▪ **CHAPTER SEVEN** ▪
UNIX Communications:
Networking, Electronic Mail,
and the Internet

UNIX has an inherent networking capabilities, which means that your capabilities can extend far past the strictures of your terminal. Indeed, depending on your level of connectivity, you can begin by sending electronic mail to other users to sending electronic mail to users across the world through the Internet. Topics covered in this chapter include:

▲   An overview of UNIX's network capabilities

▲   Using the **news** command to check the system news

▲   Finding about other users with the **who**, **rwho**, and **finger** commands

▲   Communicating directly with another user with the **write** and **talk** commands

▲   Sending and receiving electronic mail with **mail** or **mailx**

▲   Using Internet mail addresses

▲   Capturing the power of the Internet

▲   Sending electronic mail across the world

▲   Learning from the global Usenet

▲   Grasping the rules of the 'Net

▲   Grabbing remote files with the **ftp** command

▲   Uncompressing compressed files with the **uncompress** and **unpack** commands

Extending Your Powers With Networking and Communications

One area where UNIX differs dramatically from DOS is networking. DOS was meant from the beginning to serve the needs of a single user on a single machine. UNIX, on the other hand, was meant from the start to serve the needs of many users on a single UNIX system. And while these intentions have shifted slightly over the years—more and more DOS users are being connected through tools like Novell *NetWare* and Microsoft *Windows for Workgroups*—by and large both operating systems still conform closely to their roots.

Therefore, an entirely new aspect of computing is available to the DOS user who moved to a UNIX system. Things like networking and electronic mail are part of most UNIX systems, while the Internet and other extended communications play a large role in UNIX computing.

Learning About Your Network

Even if your UNIX system isn't linked to the rest of the world, its networking commands and capabilities still can be of great use to you.

The News Command

The **news** command is used to read a message that is posted for all users to read.

If there is new news on the system, you'll see the following command when you login:

```
New news
TYPE "news" to READ news
```

The usefulness of the **news** command turns directly on the ambitiousness of your system administrator. If he or she wants to send a lot of information to the users, you'll see a lot of news posted to the system. On the other hand, if your system administrator is swamped by the demands of users, they probably won't have time to post new news regularly.

As you might expect, you'd use the following command line to read the news:

```
$ news
```

The new news items will then scroll by, one page at a time.

To read all of the news items—even older items that you've already read—use the following command line:

```
$ news -a
```

To see a list of the new news items, use the following command line:

```
$ news -n
```

If there's more than one new news item, you'll see a listing of the new items:

```
$ news -n
news: Internet vi
```

To read a specific news item, you'd use the following command line like the following:

```
$ news vacation
```

where *vacation* is the name of the news item you want to read. All in all, the **news** command is summarized in Table 7.1, the Command Reference for the **news** command.

TABLE 7.1 COMMAND REFERENCE FOR THE NEWS COMMAND.

news *options newsitem(s)*

Purpose

The **news** command displays all news items distributed systemwide. These items are usually stored in **/usr/news** or **/var/news** and set up by the system administrator.

Options

–a Displays all of the news items.

–n Displays the names of all of the news items.

–s Displays a count of all of the news items.

How does the **news** command fit into a discussion of networking? Because there's only one text file accessed by the **news** command. All users have access to this same file, and they all use the same command to access it. The news item is a good example of a shared resource: Accessible by all, yet thrifty in its use of system resources.

Scoping Out Other Users

There are a score of UNIX commands that you can use to communicate with other users. The network allows you to address other users directly, as well.

But first, you need to know who else is using your computer system. The **who** command does just this:

```
$ who
oper        term/02    Jul 12 08:42
geisha      term/12    Jul 12 11:10
reichard    term/08    Jul 12 09:14
bert        term/11    Jul 12 08:55
ernie       term/10    Jul 12 07:15
```

This tells you who is logged on the system, along with a lot of other information you really don't need. (For instance, you really don't need to know what terminal the other users are sitting at, nor do you need to know the date and time they logged on the system.) Again, we see the complexity of the UNIX operating system—a simple command like **who** has far too many options.

The **who** command is summarized in Table 7.2.

TABLE 7.2 COMMAND REFERENCE FOR THE RWHO COMMAND.

who *options file*

Purpose

The **who** command displays the names and other information about users logged on the system.

Options

am I	Displays who you are (your username) (not available on all systems).
–a	Uses all options listed here (not available on all systems).
–b	Returns the last time and date the system was booted.
–d	Returns expired processes.
–H	Inserts column headings.
–l	Returns lines available for login.
–n*n*	Displays *n* users per line.
–p	Returns processes started by **init** that are still active.
–q	Quick who; displays only usernames.
–r	Returns run level.
–s	Returns name, line, and time fields (default).
–t	Returns the last time the system clock was updated with **clock** (not available on all systems).
–T	Returns the state of each terminal:
	+ Any user can write to the terminal.
	– Only system administrator can write to the terminal.
	? Error with the terminal (not available on all systems).
–u	Returns terminal usage in idle time.

On larger systems supporting hundreds of users, the output from the **who** command can be a tad overwhelming. In addition, the information returned by **who** can be on the cryptic side. For instance, you may want to use the **who** command to find out if Joe Smith from accounting is logged on the system. A quick use of **who** reveals the following entries:

```
$ who
...
joes        term/02   Jul 12 08:42
jsmith      term/12   Jul 12 11:10
...
```

Either one of these entries could pertain to Joe Smith. To find out more information about the specific user, you'd combine the username with the **finger** command:

```
$ finger joes
(612) 555-1212          In real life: Joe Smith
Directory: /home/joes      Shell:/bin/ksh
joes        term/02   Jul 12 08:42
```

If you use the **finger** command without an accompanying username, you'll get detailed information about every other user on the network, logged in or not.

The **finger** command is summarized in Table 7.3.

TABLE 7.3 COMMAND REFERENCE FOR THE FINGER COMMAND.

> **finger** *options user(s)*
>
> **Purpose**
>
> The **finger** command returns information about users with accounts on the system: Username, full name, terminal, terminal access, time of login, and phone number. In addition, **finger** grabs information from the user's login shell, **.plan** file, and **.project** file. Information is returned in long display or short display.
>
> The **finger** command will search for information based on a specific username or general first and last names. For instance, a search of the name of *smith* on a large system will probably yield quite a few responses. *continued*

Options

–b Long display, without information about home directory and shell.

–f Short display, sans header.

–h Long display, without information gleaned from the **.project** file.

–i Shows "idle" status: username, terminal, time of login, and idle lines.

–l Long display.

–m Match the username exactly, with no searching of first or last names.

–p Long display, without information gleaned from the **.plan** file.

–q Quick display of username, terminal, and time of login (with no searching of first or last names).

–s Short format.

–w Short format, without the user's first name.

If you wanted to learn about *everyone* logged on your network, including remote users, you'd use the **rwho** command. In fact, your first choice in tracking down users should be the **rwho** command, not the **who** command, as **rwho** gives a more complete accounting of all users, not just local users. However, some systems don't allow use of this command, to save on system resources.

The **rwho** command is summarized in Table 7.4.

TABLE 7.4 COMMAND REFERENCE FOR THE RWHO COMMAND.

> **rwho** *option*
>
> **Purpose**
>
> The **rwho** command shows who is logged on all machines on the entire network.
>
> **-a** Include all users, even those whose machines have been idle for more than an hour.

Communicating Directly With Other Users

After you figure out exactly who is logged on your network, you can choose from a set of commands and communicate directly with them over the network. This is the high-tech equivalent of CB radio: You send a message to another user on the network, and then you wait for their reply.

Almost all UNIX users have access to the **write** command, which send a direct message over the network to another user. If you've got a beef with the aforementioned Joe Smith after he disallowed some of your more creative expense accounts, you can drop him a nasty note directly via the following command line:

```
$ write joes
```

His computer's bell will ring (well, not actually a bell, but more like a buzzer—but UNIX still refers to it as a bell), and he'll see a message on his screen, announcing your intentions. If he wants to receive a message from you, he can respond by typing the following command line:

```
$ write reader
```

where your name is *reader*. You are free to type away, and the words you type will be visible only on his terminal and your terminal. When you end a message, type *o-o* (for *over-and-out*) and then type **Ctrl-D** (the tradition UNIX method for ending programs) and you'll be returned to your work.

The **write** program is summarized in Table 7.5.

TABLE 7.5 COMMAND REFERENCE FOR THE WRITE COMMAND.

> **write *user tty***
>
> **Purpose**
>
> The **write** command sends a text message to another user. Use **Ctrl-D** to exit.
>
> **Options**
>
> *None.*

The **write** command is meant for a single message, not an ongoing dialogue.

If you're using a newer version of UNIX, you can use the **talk** command to converse with another user.

After you run **talk** on a command line, your screen is split into two halves. The top part of the screen displays your messages, while the bottom half displays the responses from your correspondent.

To start the **talk** program, use a command line like the following:

```
$ talk joes
```

Joe Smith will see a message on his screen that looks something like this:

```
Message from Talk_Daemon@spike at 08:35
talk: connection requested by reader@spike
talk: respond with: talk reader@spike
```

where your username is *reader* and your system's ID is *spike*.

The **talk** command is summarized in Table 7.6.

TABLE 7.6 COMMAND REFERENCE FOR THE TALK COMMAND.

talk *username[@hostname] terminal*

Purpose

The **talk** command allows you to carry on a conversation with another user on the network. The command splits your screen into two areas: The top half contains your typing, while the bottom contains messages from the other user.

The **write** command is similar, except that **write** is geared for single messages and not for an ongoing dialog.

Use **Ctrl-D** to exit.

Options

user	Other user, obviously.
hostname	The *hostname* of the machine the *user* is logged on, if the user isn't logged in to your local machine.
terminal	Specified a *tty* should the *user* be logged on more than one terminal.

If *joes* doesn't want to communicate with you or anyone else, he can run the **mesg** command, which grants or denies permission to inquiring users on the network. For instance, if *joes* doesn't want to talk with anyone, he can run the following command line:

```
$ mesg -n
```

There's not a lot to the **mesg** command, as shown in Table 7.7.

TABLE 7.7 COMMAND REFERENCE FOR THE MESG COMMAND.

mesg *options*

Purpose

The **mesg** command grants or denies permission to other users to send you messages via the **write** or **talk** commands.

Options

–n   Forbids messages.

–y   Allows messages.

Electronic Mail

Electronic mail may not be the flashiest of UNIX applications, but it is certainly one of the handiest. You can send electronic mail to anyone on your network, or else you can send it to other computer users, as long as they are connected to the Internet.

▲ **L E A R N   M O R E   A B O U T** ▲

You'll learn more about the Internet later in this chapter.

As a DOS and/or *Windows* user, you may already be familiar with electronic mail, especially if you've been working on a network. But other networking systems—such as the popular DOS network software, *NetWare*—lack the basic ability to manage electronic mail and do so only after the addition of more expensive third-party packages, like *cc:Mail* or Microsoft *Mail*.

Indeed, electronic-mail capabilities have been an important part of UNIX since its humble beginnings. As UNIX has evolved, so has electronic mail—especially popular electronic-mail UNIX programs like **mail**, **mailx**, **mush**, **Mail**, and **elm**. While the exact procedures differ from program to program, the concepts underlying UNIX electronic mail remain the same. In this chapter, the **mail** and **mailx** programs will be used to illustrate electronic mail. While your electronic-mail package may differ on some of the details, broadly speaking it should work similarly to the steps outlined in this chapter.

You won't need to set up or configure your **mail** program, no matter what it may be. Check with your system administrator about the specific steps you'll use to send and receive mail on your system.

This is technical

Receiving Your Mail

When you login your system, you are told whether or not you have electronic mail waiting for you. If there is mail waiting, you'll see a line like the following:

```
You have mail.
```

This message will appear every time you login and there is mail waiting for you, as the shell is normally set up to remind you that there's electronic mail waiting.

Command

To view this mail, you'll use the **mail** command:

```
$ mailx
mail version 4.2  Type ? for help
"/var/mail/kevin": 1 message 1 new
>N 1 geisha   Wed May 18 15:18   12/227   stuff
 N  2 kreichard@mcimail.com  Wed May 18 01:13
 5/35 notes
?
```

As you can see, the system lists your electronic-mail messages in the order they were received by the system, newest mail first. The listings include the sender of the mail (in this case, *kevin*), the time and date the message was received (*Wed May 19 15:18*), the number of lines in the message and the size of the message in bytes (*12/227*), and the subject of the message (*stuff*).

If you want to read the first message listed, you'd press the **Enter** key. The entire text of the message will scroll by—probably too fast for you to read on the fly. To read a portion at a time, type **Ctrl-S**; to start the scrolling again, type **Ctrl-Q**.

In this case, there are two electronic-mail messages awaiting for you. The first, from *geisha*, was sent to you from within your own system. The second, from *kreichard@mcimail.com*, was sent from outside your system. How can you tell the difference?

Simple. If your UNIX system is connected to the Internet, you can send and receive electronic-mail messages from around the world. Mail from other systems has its own unique addressing scheme, seen here by the foreign-looking *kreichard@mcimail.com*. Mail from your own system uses the same usernames that have been explained throughout this book. Assuming your username is *geisha* and your UNIX system name is *spike*, a message sent to another user within your own system would be from *geisha*, but a message sent over the Internet would be from *geisha@spike.com*.

The question mark (?) at the end of the mail is the prompt for the **mail** program. Many UNIX commands have their own prompt. This is to make sure that you know that anything you type is meant as input for the command and not for the system as a whole.

After you've read through the messages, there are a number of actions to take by entering a letter at the **mail** command prompt. The important actions are listed in Table 7.8.

TABLE 7.8 MAIL COMMANDS AT THE MAIL PROMPT.

Command	Action
Return key	Displays the next message.
–	Displays the previous message.
?	Lists available commands.
n	Displays message *n*, where *n* in the number of a message.
d	Deletes current message; if you don't delete the message, it will be stored in the UNIX filesystem and referred to every time you use the **mail** command.
f *file*	Reads mail messages in *file*.

continued

Command	Action
h	Displays a list of messages in your mailbox.
m *address*	Creates a mail message and sends it to the electronic-mail *address*.
n	Displays the next message.
p	Redisplays the current message.
q	Quits **mail**.
r	Replies to the sender of the current message.
R	Replies to the sender of the current message, as well as other recipients of the message.
s *file*	Saves the full message to the filename *file*; if no filename is specified, the message is saved to **$HOME/mbox**.
u *n*	Undeletes message number *n*.
w *file*	Saves the message sans header to the filename *file*; if no filename is specified, the message is saved to **$HOME/mbox**.
x	Quits **mail**, but does so without deleting the messages you deleted.

Saving Your Messages

Once you've received a message, you'll probably want to save it for future reference. To do so, you need only type *s* at the **mail** command prompt:

? s

If you don't specify a filename, the system will automatically append the message to the file **$HOME/mbox**. If you don't receive many messages, it's no big deal to combine your messages into one large file. However, if you receive many mail messages on a variety of topics, then you'll want to put a little more thought into organizing your mail messages. For instance, if you're corresponding with an important client—oh, let's say the giant computer firm HAL—you may want to save all of this correspondence to a single file—say, named **HAL**. To do so, use the following **mail** command line after you read a message from a HAL executive:

```
? s HAL
```

When you do this the first time, the **mail** program creates a file named **HAL**. After that, the **mail** program will append messages to the existing **HAL** file. To read this file, use the *–f* option to the **mail** command:

```
$ mail -f HAL
```

When you save your electronic mail to a file, don't assume that the file is private, either technically or morally. The system administrator has the power to read **$HOME/mbox** and can override any file protections you may set up on the file. In addition, the courts have held that electronic-mail messages are not automatically private correspondence, and as such can be read at any time by company officials. While you shouldn't be using company resources for personal use—and we all know *that* never happens, nudge, nudge, wink, wink—be warned that you should remove any incriminating evidence should you do the unspeakable.

The Internet

An amorphous collection of networks scattered around the world, the Internet is quite the hot trend in popular culture—all thanks to UNIX, since it was the UNIX operating system that first provided the means for the Internet.

UNIX insiders may brag about being on the 'Net, but what actually constitutes the 'Net depends on the user and the system configuration. For some, being on the Internet is merely a matter of being able to send and receive electronic mail. For others, being on the Internet is a matter of receiving a news feed from the Usenet. And for others, being on the Internet means having the ability to directly connect to another computer on the Internet through UNIX tools like **ftp** and **telnet**.

The Usenet

The Usenet is a public network of computers (both UNIX and non-UNIX) that encompasses both electronic mail and **newsgroups**, which are discussion groups devoted to a single topic. The topics of the newsgroup is generally apparent from the name of the newsgroup. They are broken down into major categories, as shown in Table 7.9.

TABLE 7.9 THE MAJOR USENET NEWSGROUP CATEGORIES.

Name	Subject
alt	Alternative hierarchy; these groups are not subject to the normal rules of the Usenet
comp	Computing
misc	Miscellaneous subjects
news	News about the Usenet itself
rec	Recreational activities, such as music
sci	Science
soc	Social issues
talk	Talk

If your workplace receives a Usenet feed, you still may not have all of the newsgroups available. Many system administrators limit the number of newsgroups for two reasons: Most are rather irrelevant (such as **alt.supermodels**) and too many newsgroups can occupy some serious hard-disk space.

These classifications are broken down into more specific topics. Some typical newsgroups are listed in Table 7.10.

TABLE 7.10 SOME TYPICAL USENET NEWSGROUPS.

Newsgroup	Subject
alt.barney.die.die.die	A dislike of a purple dinosaur
comp.unix.questions	Questions about the UNIX operating system
rec.music.gaffa	The music of Kate Bush
sci.space.shuttle	Space exploration and the NASA space-shuttle program

People who have used the Usenet extensively often refer to the "signal-to-noise" ratio of newsgroups. Essentially, a good newsgroup has a high signal-to-noise ratio; there's a lot of useful information to be gathered, while the amount of meaningless blather is kept to a minimum. (In this regard, moderated newsgroups—that is, newsgroups overseen by a central authority who vets postings—are exemplary in their signal-to-noise ratio.) On the other side, most newsgroups that begin with **alt** are relatively void of any meaningful information: Lots of meaningless discussions that feature lots of angry messages from angry people. (This is not true across the board, although it doesn't take a brain surgeon to figure out that newsgroups named **alt.sex.bizarre.bestiality** or **alt.barney.die.die.die** won't add a lot to your daily living.)

The Usenet is most useful as a source of detailed technical information. Many experts in the computer world are more than happy to share their expertise with you, provided that you frame the discussion in proper terms and post your query in the proper forum.

Netiquette: Knowing the Rules

As a DOS user, you'll probably be shocked by the tone of discourse that passes for discussion on the Internet, particularly if you decide to muck around the **alt** newsgroups. These tips should assist your transition as you plumb the depths of cyberspace:

▲ Often, personal attacks pass for discourse on the Internet. These attacks are known as "flames." Ignore them. Internet geeks resort to flames when they have nothing meaningful to add to the discussion.

▲ Usenet newsgroups don't exist so you can avoid doing any work on your end. If you have a question, make sure you read the documentation or other manuals before asking your question. Many newsgroups also create Frequently Asked Questions, or FAQs, that address basic information; FAQs are posted to the group regularly. A common response to an inappropriate posting is *RTFM*, short for *Read The F_____g Manual*.

▲ You can rest assured that some net geek will attack you for being a new user. Ignore the attack. Everyone at some point was a new user.

Remote Access with Ftp

Depending on your version of UNIX and your system setup, you may have full access to the Internet, which allows you to communicate directly with any other Internet-connected computer in the world. (Your system administrator should be able to tell you if you have this capability.) The beauty is that the actual mechanisms for connecting to this remote computer are completely transparent to you, the user; all you need to do is know the remote address, and off you go.

The biggest plus to this is the ability to move files from a remote computer to your computer. In computer parlance, this is called *downloading* a file. To do so, you'll make use of two UNIX commands: **ftp** and **telnet**.

Ftp

The **ftp** command connects you to any other computer on the Internet. These computers may or not be using the UNIX operating system, but from your viewpoint it really doesn't matter. What's important is that both machines can use the **ftp** command.

Ftp stands for *file transfer protocol*. It is *interactive* software, which means it asks you for information at specific times. To run **ftp**, you type it on a command line:

```
$ ftp
ftp>
```

Like the **mail** command, the **ftp** command features its own prompt, letting you know that it is in charge of the computing session. To get a list of available commands, use a question mark (**?**) at an **ftp** prompt:

```
$ ftp> ?
```

You also can establish a direct connection to a machine either by specifying the machine's name when you begin an **ftp** session:

```
$ ftp machinename
```

or by using the **open** command after starting an **ftp** session:

```
ftp> open
(to) machinename
Connected to machinename
```

where *machinename* refers to the remote Internet-connected computer.

Reality Check: Looking for Files on the Internet

How do you know what machines to look for when you're in search for files on the Internet? Unfortunately, at this moment, the Internet is stuck in a conundrum: To look for something, you first need to know what you're looking for and where it's located. It's like trying to find a book in the library, except that the books have no information on the spines, and the card catalog isn't organized in any order.

While this situation is changing, the fact remains that you're going to get an idea of what you can get on the Internet through Usenet messages (where someone else will refer to a machine on the Internet containing specific files) or by one of the many, many Internet books on the market.

Anonymous ftp

Under most circumstances, you need an account set up on a remote machine when you use the **ftp** command. This is especially true when you deal with the commercial world. Since it's impractical to set up an account for every user in a high-traffic situation, the practice of *anonymous ftp* evolved. Instead of having an account on the remote machine, you can login the remote machine as **anonymous**. Your privileges on the machine are extremely limited—you're allowed mainly to upload and download files from a specific directory, and that's about it—but this setup works very well.

To use anonymous ftp, you'd initiate an **ftp** session in the normal way. The difference is that you'd enter *anonymous* as your name, with your electronic-mail address (referred to as your *ident*) as your password:

```
ftp> open
(to) kevin.kevinmn.com
Connected to kevin.kevinmn.com
Name (kevin.kevinmn.com): anonymous
220 Guest login ok, send ident as password.
Password: kreichard@mcimail.com
230 Guest login ok, access restrictions apply.
```

From there you'd use the regular **ftp** commands.

Let's say you know through various sources that a really cool UNIX game is stored on the machine named *kevin.kevinmn.com* (no, this isn't a real machine) in the directory named **/games**. You also know that the name of the file is **deathrow.Z**.

You would then use the following command line to connect to the machine named *kevin.kevinmn.com*:

```
$ ftp kevin.kevinmn.com
```

If the connection goes through, you'll get a message saying so, along with a login prompt. Enter *anonymous* as your name:

```
Name (kevin.kevinmn.com): anonymous
```

and then enter your full username as the password:

```
220 Guest login ok, send ident as password.
Password: kreichard@mcimail.com
```

From there you can use the remote machine as if you were using the UNIX box in your own company. To make sure that the file you want is present, you can use the **ls** command as you would if you were looking for information on your own system. You can use **cd** to maneuver through a directory structure like the structure on your own UNIX system (that is, directories and subdirectories). In addition, you'll have access to additional **ftp** commands, as listed in Table 7.11. Don't worry about doing damage when you're logged on the remote computer; you can't do any harm, and the remote system is set up so you can't accidentally erase any important files.

TABLE 7.11 COMMAND REFERENCE FOR THE FTP COMMAND.

Command	Purpose
**? *command* **	Displays help for specified *command*.
ascii	Sets transfer mode to ASCII (text) format.
bell	Create a sound (usually a beep) after a file is transferred.
binary	Sets transfer mode to binary format.
bye or **quit**	Ends ftp session and ends the **ftp** program.
cdup	Changes the current directory to one level up on the directory hierarchy; same as **cd ...**.
close	Ends ftp session with the remote machine, but continues the **ftp** command on the local machine.
**delete *filename* **	Removes *filename* from remote directory.
	continued

Command	Purpose
dir *directory filename*	Returns the contents of the specified *directory*; resulting information is stored in *filename*.
disconnect	Ends ftp session and **ftp** program.
get *file1 file2* or **recv** *file1 file2*	Gets *file1* from the remote machine and stores it under the filename *file2*; if *file2* is not specified, the *file1* name will be retained.
help *command*	Displays information about specified *command*; displays general help information if no command is specified.
mdelete *filename(s)*	Deletes *filename(s)* on the remote machine.
mdir *filename(s)*	Returns directory for multiple, specified *filename(s)*.
mget *filename(s)*	Gets the specified multiple *filename(s)* from the remote machine.
mput *filename(s)*	Puts the specified *filename(s)* on the remote machine.
open *remote_machine*	Opens a connection to the specified remote machine; if no remote machine is specified, the system will prompt you for a machine name.
put *file1 file2* or **send** *file1 file2*	Puts local file *file1* on the remote machine, under the new filename *file2*; if *file2* is not specified, the file will remain with the name *file1*.
rename *file1 file2*	Renames *file1* on the remote system to the new *file2*.
rmdir *directory*	Removes *directory* from the remote machine.

By looking at the contents of the current directory, you know that **deathrow.Z** is in the current directory. (Most anonymous ftp sites are set up so the most popular files are immediately accessible, without the need to search through directories and subdirectories.) Before you do so, you need to make sure that the **ftp** command is prepared to transfer a file like this.

The .Z tells us that the file in question is a *compressed* file. Very often, larger files will be compressed so the time needed to transfer them is minimized. How do you know that files are compressed? They end either with **.Z** or **.z**. (You've probably used compressed files at one time or another; for instance, DOS filenames ending with **.ZIP** are zipped (compressed) using the popular **PKZIP** software from PKWare.) UNIX files are compressed with two different commands: **compress** and **pack**. Files compressed with the **compress** command end with .Z, while files compressed with the **pack** command end with .z.

The commands to uncompress these files will depend on the command used to compress the files. To uncompress files compressed with the **compress** command (that is, ending with **.Z**), use the uncompress command (as shown in Table 7.12). To uncompress files compressed with the **pack** command (that is, ending with **.z**), use the **unpack** command (as shown in Table 7.13).

TABLE 7.12 COMMAND REFERENCE FOR THE UNCOMPRESS COMMAND.

uncompress *option file(s)*

Purpose

The **uncompress** command does exactly what the name says: It uncompresses a compressed file. These files usually have a name ending in **.Z**. When used, the newly compressed files will replace the original compressed file.

Option

–c   Uncompress without changing original *file(s)*.

TABLE 7.13 COMMAND REFERENCE FOR THE UNPACK COMMAND.

> **unpack** *file(s)*
>
> **Purpose**
>
> The **unpack** command unpacks a file shrunk with the **pack** commands. These files usually end with **.z**.
>
> **Options**
>
> *None.*

Anyway, to get to the reason for explaining compressed files: If a file is compressed, you must make sure that the **ftp** command knows this. Since the compressed file is a binary file, you must tell the **ftp** command so with the following command:

```
ftp> binary
```

Once you've done that, you can now grab the **deathrow.Z** file with the following command:

```
ftp> get deathrow.Z
```

When the file is transferring, there's no prompt, and the system won't accept your keystrokes. After the file has been transferred to your system, the system will tell you so in this manner:

```
Transfer complete
```

When you're done transferring files, use **bye** or **quit** to end the **ftp** command:

```
ftp> bye
```

This Chapter in Review

▲   A primary reason for UNIX's continued popularity is its ability to support many users on a network. You have many tools for making use of this network—tools that should prove quite new to you as a user of DOS, which is not usually networked.

▲   For instance, you have a few commands, such as **who** and **rwho**, that let you find out who else is logged on the network. If you want additional information about anyone on the network, use the **finger** command.

▲   You can also communicate directly with anyone on the network, using the **write** or **talk** commands. If you don't want to chat with another user, use the **mesg** command to deny all chat requests.

▲   The UNIX network also supports electronic mail, either within the network or to the rest of the world.

▲   Your company may also feature a direct connection to the Internet. If so, you have access to extended electronic mail, Usenet newsgroups, and **ftp** access.

▲   Many files available on the Internet end with a suffix of .z or .Z, which means that they are compressed (which minimizes the time needed to transfer them from site to site). If you run across a file like this, you'll need to use the **unpack** or **uncompress** commands to uncompress the compressed files.

▲   The **ftp** command allows you to grab files from the Internet. Some ftp sites require a password, while others allow anonymous access.

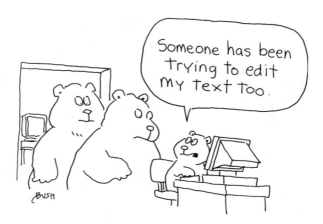

▪ CHAPTER EIGHT ▪
Text Editing and Printing

L ike DOS and *Windows*, the UNIX operating system features several tools for creating and editing text. However, these tools, like **vi** and **spell**, differ considerably from text-editing tools found in DOS and *Windows*. Topics in this chapter include:

▲ Using **vi**, the *visual editor*

▲ Comparing DOS/*Windows* and UNIX text editors

▲ Other UNIX text editors

▲ Using command and insert modes in **vi**

▲ Editing text

▲ Yanking and inserting text

▲ Moving around **vi**'s screen

▲ Checking word spellings with the **spell** command

▲ Checking word counts with **wc**

▲ Printing files with **lp**

▲ Canceling print requests

▲ Checking on print requests with **lpstat**

▼

Text Editing and Printing in UNIX

Working with text is one of the most important chores of the operating system. If you're a DOS user, you've surely worked with the primitive DOS **EDLIN** or the more sophisticated **EDIT** commands. These commands allow you to create and edit a DOS text file, which can then be used in a variety of way: As a batch file, as input for electronic mail, and so on. *Windows* users have access to the same thing with the Notepad application, as shown in Figure 8.1.

```
┌─────────────────────────────────────────────────────────┐
│ ─              Notepad - (Untitled)               ▼  ▲   │
├─────────────────────────────────────────────────────────┤
│ File  Edit  Search   Help                                │
│ This is the Windows Notepad in action.              ↑   │
│ This is the Windows Notepad in action.                   │
│ This is the Windows Notepad in action.                   │
│ This is the Windows Notepad in action.                   │
│ This is the Windows Notepad in action.                   │
│ This is the Windows Notepad in action.                   │
│ This is the Windows Notepad in action.                   │
│ This is the Windows Notepad in action.                   │
│ This is the Windows Notepad in action.                   │
│ This is the Windows Notepad in action.                   │
│ This is the Windows Notepad in action.                   │
│ This is the Windows Notepad in action.                   │
│ This is the Windows Notepad in action.                   │
│ This is the Windows Notepad in action.                   │
│ This is the Windows Notepad in action.                   │
│ This is the Windows Notepad in action.                   │
│ This is the Windows Notepad in action.                   │
│ This is the Windows Notepad in action.              ↓   │
│ ←                                                   →    │
└─────────────────────────────────────────────────────────┘
```

FIGURE 8.1 The Windows Notepad.

UNIX users also rely on text editors to create and edit files for a wide variety of uses, ranging from system configuration files (such as the **.profile** file, which has been referred to repeatedly throughout the course of this book) to input for electronic mail. UNIX offers several text-editing tools. The tool that ships with almost every UNIX system is **vi**, which is short for visual editor.

Vi takes over your entire screen and allows to view a full screen of text. It also features some rudimentary editing features, such as searching and cut and paste. While **vi** isn't the greatest text editor in the world, it certainly is functional enough for most users.

▼

Vi is not the only text editor available for the UNIX operating system. There's an older text editor called **ed**, which is almost as old as UNIX itself. While some old-time UNIX gurus argue that **ed** is still a good text editor, don't believe them—**ed** bears an uncanny resemblance to the DOS **EDLIN** command, where you essentially edit text one line at a time. This may be fine for small chores, but why bother with such an archaic tool when you have more powerful tools at your disposal?

Another popular UNIX text editor is **emacs**, from the Free Software Foundation. **Emacs** is a very fine text editor. However, it ships with very few UNIX systems, so most UNIX users don't have it.

Other UNIX text editors include **xedit** (for users of the X Window System) and **sed**, commercial products like **WordPerfect for UNIX** and **Island Write**, and programs specific to vendors (such as the **Editor** found in UnixWare). These products are all functional and useful, but they aren't as widely used as the ubiquitous **vi**.

Using Vi

I f you're a DOS user, you'll find that in some rudimentary ways **vi** is similar to the DOS **EDIT** command.

Both **vi** and **EDIT** are full-screen editors, as they both occupy the entire screen—making it easier to go through longer documents. They both create and edit ASCII files—that is, files containing only text and not specialized characters meant for use by programs. Neither supports formatting (bold, italic) of any kind, sending raw and unadorned characters straight to the printer. And neither will check your spelling—so if your spelling is terrible, don't look to **EDIT** or **vi** for help.

However, this is where the similarities end. While **EDIT** contains a host of features that make it easier to use (such as pulldown menus and an online-help system), **vi** can be annoying and difficult to use. You'll see this as we run through a typical **vi** session.

There are two ways to start **vi**: With a file loaded, or without a file loaded (where you're starting a new file from scratch). To start **vi** without a file loaded, use it as the only element on a command line:

```
$ vi
```

To start **vi** with a file loaded, use a command line like this:

```
$ vi filename
```

where *filename* refers to the file you want to edit. (If *filename* does not exist, **vi** will create it from scratch.)

If you start **vi** without a file specified, you'll see a mostly blank screen, with a cursor blinking on the top-left corner of the screen and a column of tilde (~), or null, characters running down the left side of the screen. These null characters tell us that there is nothing on the page (which doesn't make a whole lot of sense, once you stop and think about it), not even spaces or carriage returns (as generated by the **Enter** or **Return** keys). As you type and enter text, the null characters will disappear.

Vi's appearance at startup is shown in Figure 8.2.

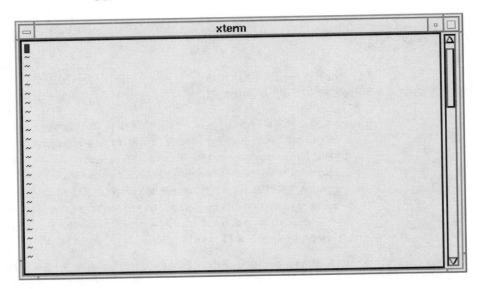

FIGURE 8.2 Vi at startup.

There are more ways to launch **vi** than with or without a file loaded, of course, as you'll see in Table 8.1, the Command Reference for the **vi** command.

TABLE 8.1 THE COMMAND REFERENCE FOR THE VI COMMAND.

vi *options filename*

Purpose

The **vi** command launches a fill-screen editor. Some versions of **vi**, most notably from Hewlett-Packard differ.

Options

–c *command*	Starts **vi** and runs *command*.
–C	Edits an encrypted file, which is a text file that has been changed for security reasons.
–L	Lists the files that were saved despite a system failure.
–r *file*	Recovers *file* after a system crash; use the **–L** command to see which files were saved.
–R	Runs **vi** in read-only mode, which means that the text cannot be changed.
–w *n*	Sets the window size at *n* number of lines.
–x	Creates an encrypted file instead of a text file, which prevents other from reading the file.
+	Starts **vi** with the cursor at the last line of the file.
+ *line*	Starts **vi** with *line* (which is a numeral) as the top line in the window.

Using Vi Modes

At this stage, you can only do one thing: enter a command. **Vi** runs in two different modes: *command* and *insert*. When you start **vi**, it's in command mode. Anything you type will be assumed to be a command by **vi**.

This is usually where you become very frustrated with **vi**, as most of your keystrokes will end up generating a series of annoying beeps unless you happen to hit upon a command. And being in command mode won't do a lot for you, especially if you're starting a file from scratch.

To get into insert mode, you'll want to hit the *i* key. At this point, you can begin editing text.

Working With Text in Insert Mode

Vi gives you exactly what you type in. For instance, if you begin typing a long line, **vi** will continue to enter the text on a single line, even after you've scrolled off the edge of the screen. If you want a line to end, you'll need to hit the **Return** key at the end of the line.

As you work with text, you'll probably be switching between command and insert modes. The **i** command isn't the only command that places you in insert mode, but the remainder makes little sense when you're working with a blank screen. As you work with text, you'll find that some of the other tools for switching to insert mode make more sense than the **i** command. For instance, the **I** command places the cursor at the beginning of the current line, not at the point where you entered command mode. Similarly, the **o** command inserts a new line immediately after the current line.

The more useful commands for entering insert mode are listed in Table 8.2.

TABLE 8.2 USEFUL COMMANDS FOR ENTERING INSERT MODE.

Command	Result
Enter key	Inserts a new line immediately following the current character.
i	Inserts text at the current character, or at the beginning of the screen when there is no text.
I	Inserts text at the beginning of the current line.
a	Appends text to the right of the current character.
A	Appends text at the end of the current line.
o	Inserts a new line immediately following the current line.
O	Inserts a new line immediately before the current line.

Command Mode

Command mode is exactly what the name implies: It's where you enter commands. At this point, you're not entering commands for the UNIX system to use (as you would at a command line), but rather only for **vi** to use. An example: **Vi** does not tell you which mode you're in—at least, not without a little prompting from you.

To switch to command mode, press the **Esc** key. If you're not sure which mode you're in, go ahead and press the **Esc** a few times—when you're in command mode and press the **Esc** key, all **vi** does is beep at you. In command mode, you can directly enter a command at the status line (the colon at the bottom of the screen). When **vi** is in command mode, your keystrokes will appear next to the status line.

Until you're more comfortable with **vi**, you should go ahead and tell **vi** to display the current mode, using the following command line while in command mode:

```
:set smd
```

Notice the colon (:) at the beginning of this command. **Vi** commands are breathtakingly inconsistent: Some commands begin with a colon, some begin with a slash (/), while most are preceded with nothing at all. Watch the exact commands presented here, and make sure that you enter exactly what is listed.

When you switch to insert mode, **vi** will display the following message on the bottom of the screen:

```
INSERT MODE
```

There are other **vi** commands that you may find useful. Most center around rudimentary editing chores, such as searching for specific strings. To look for the word *pocket* in a document, you'd use the following command:

```
/pocket
```

As always, case counts. The previous command won't find the word *Pocket*, for instance.

There are some other handy command-mode commands, and they are explained in Table 8.3.

TABLE 8.3 USEFUL VI COMMAND-MODE COMMANDS.

Command	Result
Esc key	Switches from insert mode to command mode.
Enter key	Moves the cursor to the beginning of the next line.
/string	Searches forward for *string*.
?string	Searches backward for *string*.

Moving Around the Screen

When **vi** was first designed, most UNIX keyboards lacked amenities like cursor keys (sometimes called arrow keys) and keys like **PageUp** (**PgUp**) and **PageDown** (**PgDn**). Without them, there was a need to combine the **Ctrl** key with other keys in order to move the cursor around the document.

While most users will find that the aforementioned movement keys work just fine when moving around a **vi** document, other users— especially touch typists who would rather use a **Ctrl**-key combination—may want to check out Table 8.4, which lists the main **vi** cursor and scrolling commands.

These commands are entered in command mode. If you're working in insert mode, don't forget to press the **Esc** key to enter command mode. However, movement keys like the cursor keys and the **PageUp** key can be used both in command and insert modes.

TABLE 8.4 USEFUL VI CURSOR AND SCROLLING COMMANDS.

Command	Result
0	Moves the cursor to the beginning of the current line.
$	Moves the cursor to the end of the current line.
h	Same as the **Left Arrow** key; useful for keyboards lacking cursor keys.
j	Same as the **Down Arrow** key; useful for keyboards lacking cursor keys.
k	Same as the **Up Arrow** key; useful for keyboards lacking cursor keys.
l	Same as the **Right Arrow** key; useful for keyboards lacking cursor keys.
w	Moves the cursor to the beginning of the next word.
*n*G	Moves the cursor to the beginning of line *n* (where *n* is a numeral).
G	Moves the cursor to the last line of the file.
n|	Moves the cursor to the beginning of column *n* (where *n* is a numeral).
Ctrl-B	Scrolls the document up one full page.
Ctrl-D	Scrolls the document down one-half page.
Ctrl-F	Scrolls the document down one full page.
Ctrl-U	Scrolls the document up one-half page.

In some UNIX documentation, the **Ctrl** key is represented by a carat (^). When used in conjunction with another key, the carat refers to the **Ctrl** key and *not* to the carat character found over the number 6 on most keyboards.

Saving Files

There are a few ways to save a file in **vi**. In command mode, you can save a file by using the following command:

`:w` *filename*

where *filename* is the name of the file to be saved. This command saves the file and leaves it on your screen, where you can further edit it.

To quit **vi** and save the current file (assuming that you've already given the file a name), use the following command:

`ZZ`

Vi will confirm that the file was saved by listing the filename (in quotation marks) along with the file's size, as measured in length (the number of lines) and characters. At this point, **vi** and your file will remain on the screen, but your familiar UNIX command-line prompt will appear at the bottom of your screen, indicating that the system is ready for your input.

There are other commands that quit **vi**, and they are listed in Table 8.5.

TABLE 8.5 COMMANDS FOR QUITTING VI.

Command	Result
:q	Quits **vi** after a file is saved; if the file has not been saved, **vi** will refuse to quit.
:q!	Quits **vi** without saving the file.
:w	Saves the file; if the file has not been saved yet, **vi** will request a filename.
:w *filename*	Saves file to *filename*.
:wq	Saves file and quits **vi**.
:x	Saves file and quits **vi**.
ZZ	Saves file and quits **vi**.

Editing Text in Command Mode

Editing text—that is, changing existing characters in a file—is probably more complicated in **vi** than it should be. Again, **vi**'s roots (that is, roots as a text editor with a limited keyboard) are showing in simple actions like deleting and editing text.

For instance, something as simple as changing a character is a more convoluted process than you ever thought possible. Changing a character is really a three-step process, amazingly enough:

1. The original character must be deleted. This means making sure the cursor is over the character to be changed, then going to command mode (by hitting the **Esc** key) and then typing **x**, which erases the character under the cursor.

2. You must return to insert mode by typing **i**.

3. Finally, you enter the new character.

There is an alternate method that accomplished the same thing, but requires the same number of keystrokes:

1. Move the cursor over the character to be changed, and then go to command mode by hitting the **Esc** key.

2. Type **rc**, where *c* refers to the new character replacing the character under the character to be changed.

3. Type **i** to return to insert mode.

Similarly, there are a host of options for deleting characters, should you find that the **Del** and **Backspace (BkSp)** characters don't work. You've already seen one in this section—the **x** command used for erasing the character under the cursor. Other useful deleting commands are listed in Table 8.6.

TABLE 8.6 USEFUL DELETION COMMANDS IN VI.

Command	Result
dd	Deletes the entire current line.
dw	Deletes word.
D	Deletes everything to the end of the current line.
:D	Deletes the current line.
:D$	Deletes everything to the end of the current line.
:U	Undoes the previous deletion.
x	Deletes the character under the cursor.

 You can add a number to the aforementioned movement commands and expand the actions associated with them. For instance, to delete six contiguous characters (beginning with the character under the cursor), use:

x6

instead of

x

You can use a numeral with most of the **vi** commands listed in this chapter. However, numerals tend to be most useful when deleting and editing text.

There's one more **vi** editing function you may find useful. If you want to change the case of a letter, you can avoid the rigmarole of deleting characters and inserting new characters. Place your cursor over the character to be changed, go to command mode by pressing **Esc**, and then press the tilde (~) key. This changes the case: Lowercase to uppercase and uppercase to lowercase.

Cutting and Pasting Text

Vi also features a *very* rudimentary cut-and-paste capability, if you want to remove text from one portion of the document and then insert it into another part of the document. In **vi**, this is a three-step process: Yank, position, paste.

To yank a word, move to the beginning of the word, go to command mode (by pressing the **Esc** key), and then type:

yw

You can yank characters, words, sentences, or lines. Other yank options are listed in Table 8.7.

To position, move your cursor to the point where you want to insert the yanked text.

To paste, press **p** to insert the text to the right of the cursor, and press **P** to insert text to the left of the cursor. (As always, case counts in UNIX.)

TABLE 8.7 COMMON YANKING OPTIONS IN VI.

Command	Yanks
y	the character under the cursor
y*n*	*n* number of characters
yw	the current word
yy	the current line
***n*yy**	*n* lines of text
y$	to the end of the line
y)	to the end of the sentence
y}	to the end of the paragraph
Y	the current line

Other Text-Editing Tools

There are a number of UNIX commands that complement **vi** when it comes to creating documents. This merely extends the UNIX philosophy of using specialized tools for many different tasks.

This section features some of those useful tools that can be used in conjunction with **vi**.

Using Spell

The **spell** command checks the spelling in a text file against a database of words contained within the UNIX system. The text file doesn't need to be created in **vi**.

There's no counterpart to the **spell** command in DOS, interestingly enough; DOS applications are assumed to provide their own spelling checkers if the need arises.

If a word doesn't appear in the database, the **spell** command will return the word to the screen.

To run **spell** on a file, use the following command line:

```
$ spell filename
```

where *filename* is the name of the file to check. Depending on the misspelled words, of course, the output will look something like:

```
$ spell report
Taht
spel
depnds
relevent
$
```

In this case, there are only a few misspelled words. However, if you're using the **spell** command on a larger file, you'll probably generate many more misspellings, so you'll want to redirect the output of the command to a file:

```
$ spell report > errors
```

To view this file, you can use the **vi** editor, or you can use **cat**.

Before you rely heavily on the **spell** command, you should know about the limitations associated with the command. **Spell** compares words in your original text file against a database of correctly spelled words—and to be honest, the database found in most UNIX systems isn't exactly the most complete database of words available. You'll find many words returned by **spell** as being misspelled because they don't appear in the database, even though they are spelled correctly. Also, because **spell** doesn't actually check for spelling, this command will not suggest correct spellings to "misspelled" words.

The **spell** command is summarized in Table 8.8.

TABLE 8.8 COMMAND REFERENCE FOR THE SPELL COMMAND.

spell *options files*

Purpose

The **spell** command lists "incorrectly" spelled words—that is, words not contained in a file of correctly spelled words—in a text file.

Options

–b	Checks for spellings based on British usage.
+*filename*	Creates a sorted file (in this case, *filename*; the usage is purely arbitrary) of correctly spelled words.

Using Wc

The **wc** command does one thing: It counts the number of words in a text file.

Again, in DOS, there's no analogy for the **wc** command; checking the size of a file is a function served by applications, not the operating system.

For example, the following command line lists the number of lines (10), words (55), characters (332), and the filename (report):

```
$ wc report
10 55        332 report
```

The **wc** command is summarized in Table 8.9.

TABLE 8.9 COMMAND REFERENCE FOR THE WC COMMAND.

wc *options file(s)*

Purpose

The **wc** command counts the number of words, characters, and lines in a text file.

Options

–c   Prints only the number of characters.

–l   Prints only the number of lines.

–w   Prints only the number of words.

Printing Files

In DOS, the **PRINT** command will print a file to the printer.

However, most DOS users don't use the **PRINT** command to print a document. Instead, DOS—as well as *Windows*—relies on individual applications to print their own files. DOS sends files directly to the printer, while *Windows* sends print requests to the Print Manager, which in turn sends the documents to the printer.

The UNIX method of printing is more like the *Windows* model than the DOS model. Since UNIX has to manage the needs of many users, it must also keep track of the many print requests sent by a score of users.

This is technical

You don't need to worry about exactly how UNIX manages printing. Setting up a printer for a UNIX system—especially a larger UNIX system—is a complicated task that's best left up to system administrators. In this section, we'll assume that your printer is properly configured.

However, you should review your printer arrangements with your system administrator before printing any files.

While some UNIX applications do handle their own printing, other UNIX commands—such as the **vi** text editor—rely on the operating system to print files. In these cases, you'll want to use the **lp** command.

 Some UNIX systems use the **lpr** command instead of the **lp** command. The instructions in this section can be applied to either the **lp** or **lpr** commands, for the most part. Be warned that the **lp** command is not implemented uniformly across UNIX platforms and installations, so your particular printer situations might be different. Check with your system administrator regarding what print command your system uses and what options are supported.

The **lp** command is summarized in Table 8.10.

TABLE 8.10 COMMAND REFERENCE FOR THE LP COMMAND.

lp *option(s) file(s)*

Purpose

The **lp** command sends a print request to the printer, consisting of a single file or multiple files.

Options

–c	Copies the file to a print spooler before sending the request.
–d *printer*	Specifies a printer other than the default printer.
–H *action*	Prints according to one of these actions (not available on all systems):
	hold — Suspends current or pending print jobs.
	immediate — Prints immediately after the current job is completed.
	resume — Resumes suspended print job.
–m	Sends a mail message to the user when the file is printed.
–n *num*	Prints *num* number of copies (the default is 1).

continued

–o *options*	Sets printer-specific options:	
	cpi=*n*	Prints *n* characters per inch; **pica**, **elite**, or **compressed** can be used instead of *n*.
	length=*n*	Page length, specified in inches (*n*i), lines (*n*l), or centimeters (*n*c).
	lpi=*n*	Prints *n* lines per inch.
	nobanner	Does not print the banner page.
	nofilebreak	Does not print form feed between files.
	width=*n*	Page length, specified in inches (*n*i), lines (*n*l), or centimeters (*n*c).
–t *title*	Prints *title* banner on each page.	
–w	Sends a terminal message to the user when the file is printed.	

For example, to print a file named **letter**, you'd use the following command line:

```
$ lp letter
lp: request id is hp-211 (1 file)
```

The **lp** command tells you that the file is bring printed on the printer named *hp* and has an ID of 211.

There may be many different printers on a larger UNIX network, so you may have the option of choosing another printer. Your system administrator keeps a list of installed printers—or if not, should—for your use. To use another printer on the network, you'll need to know its name (or number), and then name it on a command line, along with the *–d* option. The following command line prints the file **letter** to a printer named laser:

```
$ lp -d laser letter
lp: request id is laser-211 (1 file)
```

To find the name of the default printer, use the *–d* option with no printer or file specified:

```
$ lp -d
lp: hp
```

When you print a file, you're actually sending the request to another UNIX file, which keeps track of all print requests and makes sure that they are printed in the order they are entered into the system. The system will actually print the file when it's good and ready. However, as you're working on a file, there may be times when you give the command to print the file and then make changes to the file. Since you can't predict exactly when the system prints the file, there's the chance that the system will print the file after you make the changes. To avoid this, you may want to always print files with the use of the –c option, which uses the original file for printing:

```
$ lp -c letter
lp: request id is hp-2111 (1 file)
```

After this, you can go ahead and make changes to the **letter** file; they won't appear in what you print.

Canceling Print Requests

When you use the **lp** command, you'll notice that the system assigned an ID to the request. You can use this information to cancel the print request, should you change your mind or discover that another user has sent a *monster* 500-page document to the printer, thus keeping it occupied for a while.

The following command line will cancel the print request made in the previous section:

```
$ cancel hp-211
request "hp-211" canceled
```

If you don't remember the ID of a print request, you can use the **lpstat** command to generate a list of print requests. Actually, you may have many occasions to use this command. For instance, the **lpstat** command can warn you about the existence of the monster 500-page document. Armed with this information, you'll know that you should be sending your request to a different printer, or else be prepared to wait patiently for your request to be honored.

You can use the **lpstat** command with no options:

```
$ lpstat
hp-122 kevin      1123 May 1 11:29 on hp
hp-199 geisha 1000009 May 1 11:32
```

In this case, you can see the ID numbers for two print requests (122 and 199), that *kevin* and *geisha* have sent files for printing, the size of the files in bytes (*kevin*'s modest 1123-byte file versus *geisha*'s 1000009-byte file), the time the request was made (in this case, *kevin* was very lucky to get his print request in before *geisha*), and the status of the request (the actual printing of which is marked with the *on* notation).

The **lpstat** command is summarized in Table 8.11.

TABLE 8.11 COMMAND REFERENCE FOR THE LPSTAT COMMAND.

lpstat *options*

Purpose

The **lpstat** command lists the status of print requests, either individually or systemwide.

Options

–d Shows the name of the default printer.

–r Shows whether the print scheduler (or print spooler) is on or off.

–R Shows the position of a job in the queue (not available on all systems).

–s Summarized print status.

–t Shows all status information for all print requests.

▼

This Chapter in Review

▲ Text editing in UNIX is different than text editing in DOS and *Windows*. Tools like the DOS **EDIT** command and the *Windows* Notepad have no counterparts in UNIX. Instead, UNIX users have the choice of many lesser text-editing tools. The most common and most usable text editor in the UNIX world is **vi**.

▲ **Vi** works in two different modes: command (where you enter commands) and insert (where you edit text). Because **vi** was written at a time when most UNIX keyboards were severely limited, it relies on a number of keyboard combination to perform most basic tasks. This includes keystrokes for moving through a document, as well as for performing most basic editing tasks.

▲ The **spell** command compares the words in a file against a database of correctly spelled words. While this can be a handy tool, the limitations of **spell** dictate that you not totally rely on this command.

▲ The **wc** command tallies the number of words in a file, as well as the number of characters in the file.

▲ Most UNIX commands, such as **vi**, don't print documents directly. Instead, the resulting files from these commands are sent to the printer via the **lp** (or **lpr**) command.

▲ Commands associated with the **lp** command include the **cancel** command, used to cancel print requests, and **lpstat**, used to monitor the status of all print requests across the UNIX system.

▼

▪ CHAPTER NINE ▪
Basic Shell Programming

Advanced DOS users rely on batch files to extend the power of the operating system. UNIX features a direct counterpart in the form of shell scripts, which send a series of commands directly to the shell. This chapter is a brief overview of shell scripts and includes coverage of:

▲ DOS batch files

▲ Basic shell scripts

▲ How shell scripts work

▲ How different shells treat scripts

▲ Using scripts in the Bourne shell

▲ Creating a script

▲ Including comment lines in a script

▲ How the shell treats commands within the script

▲ Making the script executable

▲ Running a script

▲ Adding more functionality to your scripts

Automating Your Tasks
With Shell Programming

Ambitious DOS users know about *batch files*, which are used to automate various tasks. These tasks can be as unassuming as launching a program (in this case, the filename is **Q.BAT**, and it is used to launch *Quicken*):

```
cd D:\quicken
q.exe %1 %2 %3
cd\
```

or it can be elaborate as the average **AUTOEXEC.BAT** file (shown in Table 9.1) used when a DOS PC is booted.

TABLE 9.1 AN AVERAGE AUTOEXEC.BAT FILE ON A DOS SYSTEM.

```
@echo off
rem AUTOEXEC.BAT--OmniBook startup file for drive C
rem To install SMARTDrive for hard disk, remove the "rem"
rem from the smartdrv command line. The command line
rem specifies no read or write caching for drive A or B,
rem and only read caching for drive C.
rem d:\windows\smartdrv.exe a- b- e
rem The PATH must include D:\ at the end to allow access
rem to MS-DOS programs and Windows programs.
path=c:\;c:\windows;c:\winword;c:\excel;c:\dos;c:\mouse;
  c:\msmail;d:\tsi;d:\;C:\WP60
prompt $p$g
set temp=c:\windows\temp
set tmp=c:\windows\temp
set mouse=c:\mouse
d:\obsetup
rem Install SHARE (required by Microsoft Mail).
d:\share
rem To install the MS-DOS mouse driver, remove the "rem"
```
continued

```
rem from the obmouse command line.
rem d:\obmouse
c:
rem Run Windows using the WIN.BAT batch file.
call d:\win
```

In this case of Table 9.1, the **AUTOEXEC.BAT** file accomplishes several things: It sets the PATH for the system to look for files, it installs other programs (such as **SHARE**), and, above all, it documents the lines in the file through comments preceded by *rem*, short for *rem*ark. (Documenting your work is very important when creating configuration files, as you'll see later in this chapter.)

The DOS batch file has a direct counterpart in the UNIX world: the *shell script*. A script is exactly what the name says: It's a series of commands carried out by the shell. Shell scripts are specific to shells (a script written for the C shell wouldn't necessarily work under the Bourne shell).

While shell scripts may be borderline programming—indeed, more elaborate scripts *are* programming—there's no reason for you to be intimidated by the notion of shell scripts, even if you didn't work with batch files on the DOS side.

This chapter will introduce the notion of shell scripts and how they can assist you in your daily work. While you won't be viewing any elaborate scripts in this chapter, you'll see the basic structure of a script. It will be up to you to further your own script-creating education; a listing of books that cover the topic in more detail is contained in Appendix A.

The examples in this chapter are written for the Bourne shell. To see what shell is running on your system, use the following command line:

```
$ echo $SHELL
```

The response will be **sh** (the Bourne shell), **csh** (the C shell), **ksh** (the Korn shell), or some other name ending in *sh*. To change your shell to the Bourne shell, use the following command line:

```
$ sh
```

▼

If you want to exit this shell and switch back to your regular shell, use the following command line:

```
$ exit
```

Creating a Script

Like a DOS batch file, a UNIX shell script is nothing more than a series of commands presented to the shell. The script ends if an error occurs, or when all of the commands in the shell are completed. The script can contain regular UNIX commands, or else they can contain commands specific to the shell.

To create or edit a script, use a text editor like **vi** (which you learned about in Chapter 8).

The Body of the Script

With the text editor running, you can go ahead and enter the text of a script. The following example will be about the simplest script you can create, yet it will illustrate how a script works.

The example script will contain a remark line and commands. These are the two most important elements of a script, and you'll find yourself returning to them often.

The remark line is for your use only; the contents of this line won't be printed to the screen, but they will be readable in a text editor. The shell knows to ignore lines that begin with #, so the remark lines will begin with this symbol:

```
# This is a basic script that returns the date.
```

The next line will combine two commands, albeit used in differing ways. One command—**echo**—merely prints information to the screen. The other command will be nested within the script text, which means it will be treated differently by the shell, as shown:

```
echo Today is: 'date'
```

As you can see, you don't need to enclose the text echoed by **echo** in quotation marks. However, you'll probably want to do so, since common punctuation marks (like ! and ?) are used by shells for various other purposes (as you'll recall from the discussion in wildcards in Chapter 4, the question mark [?] is used as a wildcard to match a single character). Because the sample script does not use any questionable punctuation, it will forego the quotation marks.

You'll also note that the **date** command was included as part of the line to be printed to the screen. The **date** command does only one thing for an average user: It returns the current time and date. When the shell runs across a command surrounded by accent marks, it knows that it should execute the command and present the output in place of the command.

Put together, the simple script looks like the following:

```
# This is a basic script that returns the date.
echo Today is: 'date'
```

After you write the script, you can save it to file. Because there's already a **date** command, you'll want to save it to another name (since, of course, **date** would have been the most obvious choice for the script name). For the purposes of this chapter, a filename of **bogus.script** will be used.

Making the Script Executable

Before you can actually use the shell script, you must essentially tell the system that the script is a file that can be executed.

As you'll recall from previous chapters, a UNIX file can be set up to be executable by using the **chmod** command (which you first learned about in Chapter 3). Start by checking the current permissions on the small **script** file:

```
$ ls -alx script
-rw-r--r-- 1 kevin users 56 Aug 08 03:13 script
```

The following command line changes the file to an executable:

```
$ chmod u+x script
```

This command line gives you, the user (marked by *u*), permission to execute the file (marked by *+x*). To make sure that the file was marked as executable, use the following command line:

```
$ ls -alx script
-rwxr--r--  1 kevin  users    56 Aug 08 03:13 script
```

Running the Script

To actually run the script, you just type its name on the command line:

```
$ script
```

The end result looks like the following:

```
$ script
Today is: Tue Aug 9 10:12:14 CDT 1994
```

Obviously, this is the most simplistic and meaningless shell script that one can create, since all it does is add a few words to the output of the **date** command. There are a number of things you can do to make your own scripts more functional:

▲ **Add variables.** You've already covered variables in Chapter 5, so you know how UNIX treats them. You can add variables to a script to echo previous input or to respond differently to different input.

▲ **Loops.** Programmers know all about loops. In essence, a loop is a command that is executed over and over until a condition is met.

▲ **Redirect input/output.** You can use redirection (<, >, and so on) to redirect the input within a script to another command.

If you want to learn more about shell scripts, look to a list of recommended books in Appendix A for a suitable primer.

This Chapter in Review

▲ Many DOS users rely on batch files to automate their work. UNIX offers a direct counterpart with shell scripts.

▲ A shell script is nothing more than a series of instructions to the shell. Creating a shell script is like programming, but simple scripts are nothing as complicated as the most simple program.

▲ You can use a text editor, such as **vi**, to create and edit a shell script.

▲ Always enclose remark lines within your shell script. In addition to serving as a reminder to yourself, they also serve as a guide should someone else be called upon to use your system configuration.

▲ Commands are treated in two ways by the shell: Either as a command to be run directly, or as a command whose output should be sent to the same position within the shell script. In the latter, the command should be surrounded by accent marks.

▲ Before you run a script, you must inform the system that the file containing the script is executable. To do so, you'll use the **chmod** command and change the file permissions for the file.

▲ To run a script, you merely enter the name of the file containing the script on the command line.

▲ There are a number of ways you can make your shell script more functional, including the use of variables, loops, conditional statements, and redirection.

▪ CHAPTER TEN ▪
Disk Usage in DOS and UNIX

Your work would be pretty meaningless if you didn't have a way to store it. DOS/*Windows* and UNIX might use hard disks to store information, but the similarity ends there, as UNIX offers less control over a hard-disk system than do DOS and *Windows*. Topics in this chapter include:

- ▲ The disk responsibilities of the average user
- ▲ Knowing when to leave things up to the system administrator
- ▲ The basics of UNIX disk storage
- ▲ PC Unices and their disk arrangements
- ▲ Treating the hard disk as an extension of RAM
- ▲ Swapping processes to and from the hard drive
- ▲ Using paging to manage multiple users
- ▲ DOS commands that have no counterpart in the UNIX world
- ▲ Reporting the amount of free disk space with **df**
- ▲ Charting disk usage with the **du** command
- ▲ UNIX and floppy drives
- ▲ Making backups under UNIX

▼

Worlds Apart

So far this book has focused on the similarities between DOS and UNIX, dealing only with differences as they arise.

But you must have deduced by now that there are some serious differences between DOS and UNIX—differences that affect the very way you do your daily work. The intent of this book is to give you a gentle transition from DOS to UNIX.

One issue that you'll probably be unprepared for is the amount of control you have over the disk-storage system. As a DOS user, you're used to complete control over the entire computer. You can act as a god in system configurations and storage requirements.

The same won't be true in UNIX, unless you get a job as a system administrator—where you do indeed become a god of sorts. When a hard disk gets jammed and almost full, it's up to the system administrator to clear out some deadwood in the form of unneeded files. The average user doesn't have this responsibility, let alone the power, to make these changes.

The average user is responsible for their little corner of the UNIX filesystem. It's up to the system administrator to make sure that things are set up correctly.

UNIX Disk Storage

As a DOS/*Windows* user, you were used to total control over the hard-disk storage system. You probably had a drive C: at your disposal, and drives D: and E: as well, or even more, if you were on a network.

The first thing you'll need to learn about UNIX and disk drives is that you don't have the same flexibility when it comes to partitions and drive names. Indeed, in UNIX, there's only a single root directory. There are no partitions, and no drive names assigned. While there may be times when you need to access a remote filesystem, your system administrator should have worked out the messy details for you.

▼

This is technical

The previous information is generally true. However, the rules change slightly when it comes to PC-based Unices, especially if they feature the ability to run DOS. There, the PC UNIX will occupy its own partition on the hard-disk system. Within that partition, the PC UNIX will set up a DOS partition for storing and running DOS programs. In addition, you can set up a DOS partition on the same hard drive. This DOS partition can't be seen by the PC UNIX, but it can be seen by the DOS session running *under* the PC UNIX. (It can also be seen by DOS if the machine is booted with DOS.) This is a handy way of moving files between DOS and UNIX: The DOS running under the PC UNIX can be used to copy files to that DOS partition. After the system is rebooted running DOS, the file can then copied be from that first DOS partition.

This can lead to some very confusing situations. Since the PC UNIX must be installed at first sector of the boot drive and PC Unices occupy a good chunk of hard-disk space, you'll probably be devoting most of drive C: to the PC UNIX. It's also a good idea to throw a DOS partition on that same drive, to facilitate the file-transfer possibilities mentioned in the previous paragraph. On this author's PC, for instance, the partitions shown on Table 10.1 exist on the hard-disk system.

TABLE 10.1 UNIX/DOS PARTITIONS.

PC Partition	UNIX sees:	DOS under UNIX sees:	DOS sees:
C: UNIX 180MB	180MB	180MB	——
C: DOS 20MB	——	20MB	20MB
D: DOS 400MB	——	——	400MB

This also leads to some weird drive mappings, particularly when running DOS under UNIX. Because there are essentially three partitions on drive C: (remember, the PC UNIX maps an internal DOS partition within the UNIX partition), DOS under UNIX actually sees three drives: Drive C: (the UNIX partition), drive D: (the internal DOS partition within the UNIX partition), and drive E: (the real DOS partition). When DOS is running by itself, it sees drive C: (the 20MB DOS partition) and drive D: (which is the second hard drive).

The Needs of Many
Outweigh the Needs of One

At its core, the term multitasking means that the operating system can do more than one thing at a time. You already know that DOS and *Windows* perform only one task at a time, and you've already seen the UNIX commands that rely on multitasking. And you already know how UNIX supports multiple users on a single installation.

But you probably don't know how multitasking and multiuser affects a UNIX system. When dealing with a lot of users, the system inevitably bogs down—even slower than you've ever experienced with *Windows*.

In these cases, UNIX is using the system's disk drives as an extension of the system's random-access memory, or RAM, by *swapping* to disk. However, hard disks are much slower than RAM, and so the time spent accessing the hard drives slows down the system. (When this occurs, the system is said to *thrash*—a suitable metaphor.)

The mechanism is simple, really. When you launch a new process (either directly by launching a command or indirectly), the system attempts to load the process into an unoccupied section of RAM. If RAM is available, the process is loaded. If RAM is not available, the system looks for a process that is not running at that moment. This process is then moved to a special area of the hard disk devoted to swapping. (This procedure has a parallel in the DOS world: RAM disks. However, in the UNIX world the average user doesn't have control over the size of RAM disk, while in DOS the user has complete control.) And the process begins again.

Paging

Newer UNIX systems extend the practice in a more efficient manner through support of *paging* (also known as *virtual memory*). Instead of moving program-sized portions of RAM to and from the hard disk, a paging system moves small chunks of RAM, known as *pages*, to and from the hard disk. When you launch a process, the system searches for a page of available RAM (usually 4,096 kilobytes) and loads the beginning of your program into that page. Any additional RAM needs of your program are handled by the page, and when the page fills, another page is sought by the system.

When the system runs out of pages in RAM, it then uses the hard drive for paging. Processes aren't necessarily grouped contiguously, so one portion of the process can be pages to disk while another active portion is left in RAM. Because a portion of the process is paged—as opposed to swapping, where the entire processed is swapped in and out of disk—paging is considered more efficient than swapping.

What's the lesson in all of this? Because the hardware in a UNIX installation must serve the needs of all users, you as an ordinary user have less control over the hardware. The DOS commands that directly control the hard disk, such as **DBLSPACE**, **DISKCOPY**, and **FORMAT**, have no counterpart in the UNIX world. As an ordinary user, you don't have the power to wipe out a hard disk with the **FORMAT** command. And you don't have the ability to copy the entire contents of a disk with **DISKCOPY**. In fact, you don't even have the ability to set up a RAM disk as you do in DOS.

Disk Utilities in UNIX

There are a few tools for monitoring disk usage in UNIX, tools that have indirect counterparts in the DOS world.

Indirect? Yes. When a DOS user has a hard disk that is almost full, there are steps that must be taken. When a UNIX user has a hard disk that is almost full, the only thing to do is inform the system administrator. For instance: There are a few UNIX commands that provide the same sort of information provided by the DOS **DIR** command. One of them is **df** (disk free), which reports the amount of disk space that is currently free. The information returned by **df** looks something like this:

```
$ df
/           (/dev/root ):        75756 blocks     21797 files
/proc       (/proc        ):          0 blocks       174 files
/dev/fd     (/dev/fd      ):          0 blocks         0 files
/stand      (/dev/dsk/c0t0d0sa):   14694 blocks       194 files
```

This is technical

Here we run into some new terminology.

UNIX rarely measures disk space in bytes. Instead, the standard measure is a *block*, which is usually 512 bytes. (There's also an infrequently used variation called a *logical block* that is 1,024 bytes.)

Though UnixWare (the version of UNIX generating the previous **df** information) returns information in terms of files, most UNIX systems use *inodes* as a term of measurement. An inode is a way for UNIX to keep track of information on a disk. Indeed, you can think of an inode (short for identification node) as an index for a file, containing information about where the file is stored on the physical disk. It's the UNIX equivalent of a file-allocation table (FAT) in UNIX.

The **df** command is summarized in Table 10.2.

TABLE 10.2 **COMMAND REFERENCE FOR THE DF COMMAND.**

df *options filesystem*

Purpose

The **df** command returns the amount of free disk blocks and free inodes (or in some cases, free files) on a given filesystem. Be warned that this command differs radically from system to system.

Options

–b   Prints only the number of free kilobytes.

–e   Prints only the number of free files.

–k   Prints the returned information in kilobytes.

–l   Reports only on local filesystems.

Command

The other UNIX command that provides information similar to that returned by the DOS **DIR** command is **du**, which returns the current disk usage in terms of the existence of subdirectories. A sample of typical information provided by **du** follows:

```
$ du
4               ./.wastebasket
4               ./Utilities
2               ./mailbox
4               ./Applications
```

```
2            ./Disks-etc
0            ./Preferences/Backdrop_Library/Backdrop_Items
6            ./Preferences/Backdrop_Library
4            ./Preferences/Startup_Items
14            ./Preferences
4            ./System_Setup
4            ./Accessories
2            ./Games
6298         ./windows/system
13082        ./windows
15674        .
```

As with **df**, the disk usage is summarized in blocks (though there is an option to return information for all files, not just subdirectories). The **du** command returns the size of the directories contained within local filesystem (in this case, the local filesystem on a UnixWare system—hence the references to *Windows* and some other oddities).

The **du** command is summarized in Table 10.3.

TABLE 10.3 COMMAND REFERENCE FOR THE DU COMMAND.

> **du** *options directories*
>
> **Purpose**
>
> The **du** command lists the amount of disk usage through the size of subdirectories.
>
> **Options**
>
> **–a** Prints information for all files, not just subdirectories.
>
> **–r** Returns a message if a file or subdirectory cannot be opened.
>
> **–s** Prints the total for each directory.

▼

If you're on a single-user UNIX configuration, these kind of disk utilities can be important if you want to keep your own system running smoothly. Similarly, these commands are important to system administrators, whose jobs depend on systems running smoothly.

However, as an average user, these commands are of little more than academic interest. On a larger system, your own personal disk usage isn't going to make a huge dent in the total disk usage.

Working with Floppies

Depending on your version of UNIX, you may be able to work directly with DOS-formatted floppy disk. UnixWare, for instance, treats the disk drives of the PC in the same manner DOS does. You can copy files directly to and from the disk drives. Even though DOS and UNIX files are formatted differently, UnixWare is set up to translate a UNIX file to a DOS diskette, and vice versa.

However, this is not the rule across the board. SCO UNIX users need to *mount* a floppy drive before it can be used. (To mount a drive means to make the system aware of the drive's existence.) Workstations from Sun Microsystems, for instance, feature a floppy-disk drive, but a user must take special steps before using it as a drive that can read and write to DOS-formatted floppy disks.

If you're in doubt, check with your system administrator or documentation about using floppies on your UNIX system.

Making Backups: It's Not Your Department

Similarly, there are a few DOS commands that deal with backing up the contents of a hard disk, like **MSBACKUP** or **BACKUP**. There are counterparts in the UNIX world like **cpio** and **tar**.

Unless you're working on a single-user UNIX configuration, however, you're not expected to use these commands. Again, backing up the system is the domain of the system administrator, whose job it is to make frequent system backups. This usually takes place at a given time, and the entire filesystem is usually backed up to tape or optical storage.

▼

▼

This Chapter in Review

▲ The average UNIX user has less control over the system's hard-disk system than does the average DOS/*Windows* user.

▲ DOS utilities like **FORMAT** and **DBLSPACE** really have no counterpart in the UNIX world, since UNIX users are not expected to deal with the hard-drive system on an administrative level. This task is left up to the system administrator.

▲ For the UNIX user, there's a single root directory. There are no drive names to navigate, such as drive C: and D: in DOS.

▲ PC UNIX users, however, must deal with the drive names used by the PC hardware. When there are multiple partitions and DOS running as a task under UNIX, this can be a tricky affair.

▲ Most UNIX system grab a portion of the hard disk to be used as an extension of the system's RAM. This can take the form of swapping to disk (where an entire process is banished to the hard drive) or paging (where a portion of the RAM is sent to the hard drive). Paging is the more efficient method, but is not available on all UNIX systems.

▲ There are a few commands that monitor disk usage: **df** (*d*isk *f*ree) and **du** (*d*isk *u*sage). Unless you're working on a single-user UNIX installation, you won't get much use from these commands.

▲ Some versions of UNIX, particularly PC Unices and workstations, have the ability to work with floppy diskettes. However, the exact mechanisms for working with these floppies are unique to every system, so check with your system administrator or online-manual pages for details.

▪ APPENDIX A ▪
For More Information

This book is only the beginning of the journey, should you desire to advance your working knowledge of UNIX. This appendix lays out further sources of information.

Printed Documentation

If the documentation that came with computer systems were any good, there would be no reason for a book like this. Have you browsed through the documentation that came with your UNIX system? Ouch.

This documentation serves its purpose: It provides valuable information for the system administrator. The purpose of this documentation is not to provide illumination for the end user. While some system-specific information can be found only in the documentation, the vast amount of it is technical information geared toward the advanced user. Approach the documentation with a grain of salt: Don't feel inadequate if you don't understand it fully.

Online-Manual Pages

O ne of the neater UNIX commands is **man**, which displays information about UNIX commands.

There's not a lot to the **man** command (as you'll see from Table A.1, the Command Reference for the **man** command)—essentially, it displays an **online-manual page** about specific UNIX commands. It will not display information about practices and procedures, nor will it display information about specific UNIX topics, like *multitasking* or *processes*. Still, it's quite useful for displaying a *lot* of information about specific commands.

Unfortunately, the **man** command is not fully implemented on some UNIX system, and not at all on other UNIX systems. If you have it, great; if not, lobby your system administrator.

For more information on the **man** command itself (assuming you have access to it, of course), use the following command line:

```
$ man man
```

TABLE A.1 COMMAND REFERENCE FOR THE MAN COMMAND.

> **man** *command*
>
> **Purpose**
>
> The **man** command displays the online-manual page for a command.
>
> **Options**
>
> *None.*

Books

A s you can tell by a visit to your local bookstore, there are a ton of titles devoted to the UNIX operating system. However, when you start looking at the titles and the tables of contents, you realize that most of them are meant for advanced users and/or system administrators. By contrast, the book in your hands is one of the few books devoted to anyone other than advanced users and/or system administrators, and perhaps the only one devoted only to the UNIX neophyte.

At this point in your UNIX education, though, you may be ready to move on to more advanced tomes. Here are some titles that should aid you in your higher education.

General Titles

UNIX Fundamentals: UNIX Basics. Kevin Reichard, MIS:Press, 1994. This book is the first in this series, and it lays out the basics of UNIX usage. If you're still puzzled by some aspects of UNIX usage, this is a good place to start.

Teach Yourself UNIX. Kevin Reichard and Eric F. Johnson, MIS:Press, 1992. This introduction to the UNIX operating system is meant for a more advanced computer user, but still has enough details for the learning beginner. Most of the commands listed in this work are more fully explained in *Teach Yourself UNIX*, while the underlying concepts of UNIX are explained in depth.

UNIX in Plain English. Kevin Reichard and Eric F. Johnson, MIS:Press, 1994. This reference works focuses on in-depth explanations of the important UNIX commands. Definitely the book to be sitting next to your terminal for a quick reference.

X Window System

Using X. Eric F. Johnson and Kevin Reichard, MIS:Press, 1992. This book explains the basics of X Window System usage and configuration. While X Window can be complex, even a beginner is able to handle the very elementary configuration details, as explained in this book.

Online Sources

As you might expect from a computer system with networking built in, there are many online resources you can tap. The greatest amount of information is carried over the Usenet.

Usenet UNIX Newsgroups

The Usenet is a close cousin to the Internet, which was discussed in Chapter 7. The Usenet, however, contains only newsgroups devoted to discussion of specific topics. Be warned that many of the newsgroups are geared toward experts of one sort or another, and that some may feel that participation by a UNIX neophyte is not exactly welcome. Asking a general question of a set of UNIX experts is generally met by disdain, rudeness, and techie arrogance. (The exception is the *comp.unix.questions* newsgroup, which is designed specifically for beginners.) If you choose to participate in a specialized topic, you're on your own; the advice from these quarters is to monitor the newsgroups and pick up useful knowledge in that fashion. (In fact, many of the newsgroups feature messages called **FAQs**, or **Frequently Asked Questions**. You'll want to pay special attention to messages with this heading.) General questions are best asked of your system administrator or other UNIX users in your area.

There are many newsgroups on the Usenet devoted to UNIX topics. The list in Table A.2 comes directly from a regular compilation of Usenet newsgroups. However, be warned that Table A.2 comprises only a sampling of other UNIX-related newsgroups; other more obscure or specialized newsgroups have been omitted.

TABLE A.2 USENET NEWSGROUPS RELATING TO UNIX.

Newsgroup	Purpose
comp.unix.admin	Administering a UNIX-based system.
comp.unix.advocacy	Arguments for and against UNIX.
comp.unix.aix	A discussion of the IBM version of UNIX.
comp.unix.aux	A discussion of the Apple Macintosh version of UNIX.
comp.unix.bsd	A discussion of Berkeley Software Distribution UNIX.
comp.unix.dos-under-unix	A discussion of MS-DOS running under UNIX.
comp.unix.large	A discussion of UNIX on mainframes and in large networks.
comp.unix.misc	Miscellaneous topics.
comp.unix.osf.osf1	A discussion of the Open Software Foundation's OSF/1.
comp.unix.pc-clone.16bit	A discussion of UNIX on 80286 architectures.
comp.unix.pc-clone.32bit	A discussion of UNIX on 80386 and 80486 architectures.
comp.unix.programmer	Q&A for people programming under UNIX.
comp.unix.questions	UNIX neophytes group.
comp.unix.shell	Using and programming UNIX shells.
comp.unix.sys5.r4	A discussion of System V Release 4.
comp.unix.ultrix	A discussion of DEC's Ultrix.
comp.unix.unixware	A discussion of Novell's UnixWare products.
comp.unix.user-friendly	A discussion about UNIX user-friendliness.
comp.unix.wizards	For only true UNIX wizards (moderated).

CompuServe

There are hundreds of forums on CompuServe, but an especially friendly forum for UNIX beginners is the UNIX Forum. Topics in this forum include: Forum Info/General, New to UNIX, Communications, Networking, Applications, UNIX OS Topics, DOS under UNIX, and GUI and X Window. This forum also contains software libraries. (To get to the UNIX Forum, type GO UNIX.)

In addition, there are forums maintained by several UNIX vendors that specialize in PC versions of UNIX, and the users on these forums generally have one foot in the DOS world and one foot in the UNIX world. If you need to combine the two worlds, you might want to check out the UnixWare (GO UNIXWARE) or SCO (GO SCO) forums for some advice and pertinent software libraries.

And don't forget the existence of CompuServe forums dedicated to certain portions of UNIX usage.

▲ **L E A R N   M O R E   A B O U T** ▲

For instance, there's an Internet forum (GO INETFORUM) that you might find useful if you want to follow up on Chapter 7.

▪ **APPENDIX B** ▪
UNIX/DOS Cross Reference

T his appendix lists all the DOS commands (as of MS-DOS 6.2) and their counterparts in the UNIX world. Some of the more obscure DOS commands with DOS counterparts, such as **PAUSE** and **SLEEP**, weren't covered in the course of this book—mostly because they aren't worth any extended coverage.

Not all DOS commands have a UNIX analog, obviously. Similarly, there are some UNIX commands that simply have no parallel in the DOS world. In cases of DOS commands with no UNIX parallel, we note that situation. And not all of the commands are *perfectly* matched; in some cases, we're listing the rough equivalent.

DOS Command	UNIX Command
APPEND	*None*
ASSIGN	*None*
ATTRIB	**chmod**
BACKUP	**cpio, tar**
BREAK	*None*
CALL	**exec**
CD	**cd**
CHCP	*None*
CHDIR	**cd**
CHKDSK	*None*
CHOICE	*None*
CLS	**clear**
COMMAND	**csh, sh**
COMP	**bdiff, cmp, diff, diff3, sdiff**
COPY	**cp**
CTTY	**stty**
DATE	**date**
DBLSPACE	*None*
DEFRAG	*None*
DEL	**rm**
DELTREE	**rm –r**
DIR	**ls**
DISKCOMP	*None*
DISKCOPY	*None*
DOSKEY	**history** (Korn and Bourne shells)
DOSSHELL	*None*
ECHO	**echo**

continued

DOS Command	UNIX Command
EDIT	**vi**
EXIT	*None*
EXPAND	**uncompress, unpack**
FASTHELP	**apropos, man, whatis**
FASTOPEN	*None*
FC	**bdiff, cmp, diff, diff3, sdiff**
FDISK	**fsck**
FIND	**grep**
FOR	**for** (shell command)
FORMAT	*None*
GOTO	**goto** (C shell)
GRAFTABL	*None*
GRAPHICS	*None*
HELP	**apropos, man, whatis**
IF	**if** (shell command)
INTERLNK	*None*
INTERSVR	*None*
JOIN	*None*
KEYB	*None*
LABEL	*None*
LOADFIX	*None*
LOADHIGH	*None* (thankfully)
MEM	*None*
MEMMAKER	*None*
MIRROR	*None*
MKDIR	**mkdir**
MODE	**stty, tty**
MORE	**more, pg**

continued

DOS Command	UNIX Command
MOVE	**mv**
MSAV	*None*
MSBACKUP	**cpio**, **tar**
MSD	*None*
NLSFUNC	*None*
PATH	**setenv PATH** (C shell), **setpath** (Bourne shell)
PAUSE	**sleep**
POWER	*None*
PRINT	**pr**
PROMPT	**PS1**
RECOVER	*None*
REM	**#**
RENAME	**move**
REPLACE	*None*
RESTORE	**cpio**, **tar**
RMDIR	**rmdir**
SET	**env**
SETVER	*None*
SHARE	*None*
SHIFT	*None*
SMARTDRV	*None*
SORT	**sort**
SUBST	*None*
SYS	*None*
TIME	**date**
TREE	*None*
TYPE	**more**, **page**, **pg**

continued

DOS Command	UNIX Command
UNDELETE	*None* (unfortunately)
UNFORMAT	*None*
VER	**uname**
VERIFY	*None*
VOL	*None*
VSAFE	*None*
XCOPY	**cp**

▪ GLOSSARY ▪

absolute pathname

> The full name of a file, from the root directory on through each sub-directory.

account

> Information about your UNIX usage, such as your username and the way your terminal is configured.

address

> The name of a computer on the network or the name of the entire computer system, used in communications and electronic mail.

anonymous ftp

> Logging on a remote system anonymously to retrieve files (that is, logging in a system without having an account already set up on the system); this method involves limited access to the remote system.

append

> Attach characters to the end of an existing file.

application

A program that perform a specific task, such as a text editor or a database manager.

archive

A file that can contain one or more files, serving as a backup (usually on tape) to files on a hard drive.

arguments

Additions to a command that slightly change the result of the command, either by adding options or specifying filenames.

ASCII

American Standard Code for Information Interchange; a standard format used to store basic alphabetic characters and numerals in a way that any computer—running UNIX or another operating system—can read the file.

background

State where commands are run without the full attention and resources of the system; when the commands finish running the user is notified. Background commands are run from a command line that ends with an ampersand (&).

Bourne shell

See *shell*.

C

Programming language that serves as a basis of UNIX; in addition, most UNIX programs are written in C or its successor, C++.

C shell

See *shell*.

command

A direct instruction to the computer system.

command line

The combination of a command and any arguments to the command.

command prompt

A specific character used by a specific shell in conjunction with the cursor to tell you that the system is ready for a command.

compressed file

A file that has been shrunk so that it can more quickly be transferred from computer to computer.

current directory

Your current position on the directory tree.

cursor

A blinking line or square on the monitor that tells you the system is waiting for a command.

default

A state or value assumed when no other is present.

device

A physical device attached to the computer system, such as a modem or tape drive.

directory

The means for storing files or other directories, analogous to a folder in a file cabinet.

DOS

See *MS-DOS*.

electronic mail

The electronic equivalent of mail: text messages sent over the UNIX network, either from within the system or from outside the system.

encryption

A way of encoding a file so that it cannot be read by other users.

environment

Information that determines your UNIX usage and system configuration, as stored in your **.profile** file or set during your computing session.

error message

A message from the computer system informing you that it cannot perform a specific function.

executable file

A file containing a program.

FAQ (Frequently Asked Questions)

A list of commonly asked questions on a specific topic (and their answers, of course) disseminated via the Internet.

field

A vertical column of data from a structured data file, with all of the entries of the same type.

file

The mechanism for storing information on a UNIX system: A set of characters (called bytes) referenced by its filename.

filename

The name for a file.

filesystem

The method used in UNIX to organize files and directories: A root directory contains several subdirectories, and these subdirectories in turn may contain further subdirectories.

foreground

Commands that have the full attention of the system and do not return control of the system to the user until the command is complete. In UNIX, the default is to run commands in the foreground.

freeware

Software created by others and then given away to the computing community at large.

graphical interface

A graphical display on the monitor, with windows, scrollbars, and icons.

group

A defined set of users.

hidden files

UNIX system files that are used for standard housekeeping chores; the filenames begin with a period (.) and are not listed with the **ls** command.

home directory

A directory where your own files are stored, and where you are placed after you login the system.

hostname

The name of your UNIX system.

icon

A graphical representation of a program or file.

inbox

The storage area for electronic mail that has not been read.

Internet

The umbrella name for a group of computer networks that distribute electronic mail and newsgroups around the world.

keyboard

The big thing you type on to provide input to the computer.

Korn shell

See *shell*.

link

A file that serves as a reference to another file. Many users can use the same files, making it appear as though they each have their own copy of the file.

login

To announce your presence to the system by entering your username and password.

login shell

A script, usually contained in **.login**, that contains basic information about your UNIX usage; this script runs every time you login.

logname

The name the UNIX system uses to keep track of you. Also known as *username*.

Meta key

A specified key used in conjunction with other keys to create additional key combinations. On most keyboards, the **Alt** key is really the **Meta** key.

Microsoft *Windows*

A graphical interface that runs on top of MS-DOS.

monitor

That big ol' thing sitting on your desk that looks like a television on steroids.

multiprocessing

When more than one task can be performed simultaneously by the operating system. UNIX is a *multiprocessing* operating system.

multitasking

When more than one task can be performed simultaneously by the operating system. UNIX is a *multitasking* operating system.

multiuser

When more than one user can be using the same computer system. UNIX is a *multiuser* operating system.

MS-DOS

An operating system used by most PCs.

networking

Connecting one computer system to another computer system by direct wiring or phone lines.

online manual page

Documentation for your system stored within files on the system, accessed with the **man** command.

operating system

A program that controls all actions of the computer hardware. UNIX is an operating system.

option

Characters that modify the default behavior of a command.

ordinary file

A file that is, well, ordinary, containing data or programs, with no special characters.

OSF/Motif

Created by the Open Software Foundation, Motif is actually many things—but for you, the most important thing is that it defines a look and feel for the graphical interface. Based on the X Window System.

owner

The user with the ability to set permissions for a file.

paging

Memory-management system where small chunks of the UNIX system's RAM is switched back and forth between the hard disk. This situation occurs when there's not enough RAM to serve the needs of all users.

parent directory

The directory containing a subdirectory.

password

A unique set of character that the UNIX system uses to verify your existence when you want to login the system.

permissions

A security tool to determine who can access a file.

pipe

A conduit between two commands, which tells the second command to use the output from the first command as input.

process

Essentially, a command running on the computer.

process ID (PID)

Number assigned by the system to a command.

program

A set of instructions for the computer to carry out.

prompt

See *command prompt.*

redirection

Changing the standard input/output; for instance, saving output to a file instead of printing it to the screen.

relative pathname

A filename in relation to the current directory position.

root directory

The top-most directory on the directory tree; every directory on a UNIX system is a subdirectory of the root directory. Indicated in all pathnames as a slash (/).

root user

The user who can do just about anything possible within the UNIX operating system. Also referred to as the **superuser.**

server

A computer that supplies files and services to other computers.

shell

Software that acts as a buffer between you and the operating system. There are many different UNIX shells—the Bourne shell, the Korn shell, and the C shell, for example.

shell script

A text file that serves as a set of instructions for the shell.

special device files

Files that represent physical parts of the UNIX system, such as tape drives or terminals.

standard input/output

The UNIX method of processing commands: The standard input comes from the keyboard, and the output goes to the screen.

states

Different levels that a UNIX system runs in, ranging from a single-user state to a multiuser state.

subdirectories

A directory contained within another directory. In UNIX, every directory is a subdirectory of the root directory.

swapping

Situation where UNIX processes are sent from RAM to a hard disk for temporary storage. This arises because of a shortage of available RAM in the system.

system administrator

running and maintaining the UNIX system.

terminal

A monitor, keyboard, perhaps a mouse, and perhaps a CPU.

text-based interface

An interface where only characters, and not graphics, are used.

text file

A file containing only ASCII characters and no special characters. A text file can be read by any program.

UNIX

An operating system that supports more than one user and can perform more than one command at a time—and, of course, the greatest operating system in the world.

username

The name the UNIX system uses to keep track of you. Also known as *logname*.

variable

A symbol or character that has different meanings based on context and specific usage.

wildcard

Special characters within a filename that tells the shell to look for all files with similar filenames.

window manager

A program within the X Window System that controls the look and feel of the interface.

Windows

See *Microsoft Windows*.

working directory

See *current directory*.

workstation

A computer optimized for running UNIX. Sun SPARCstations and IBM RS/6000s are *workstations*.

X terminal

A terminal that runs only the X Window System and draws most of its computing power from the network.

X Window System

Graphical windowing system used for building graphical interfaces, like Motif.

xterm

Popular X Window System program that provides a command-line interface to the UNIX operating system.

▪ INDEX ▪

Commercial products are listed under vendor names.

A

B

C

D

H

▼

T

U

V

Date Due

12/22 '95			
DEC 1 0 1997			
MAY 5 1998			
JUL 1 4 1998			
DEC 1 3 2002			

BRODART, CO.   Cat. No. 23-233-003   Printed in U.S.A.